AF708342

The Other Side of the Airport

The Other Side of the Airport

The Private Pilot's World

BY MILTON E. BRENER

Jason Aronson/NEW YORK • LONDON

Copyright © 1982 by Milton E. Brener

10 9 8 7 6 5 4 3 2

All rights reserved. Printed in the United States of America. No part of this book may be used or reproduced in any manner whatsoever without written permission from *Jason Aronson, Inc.* except in the case of brief quotations in reviews for inclusion in a magazine, newspaper or broadcast.

ISBN: 0-87668-493-2

Library of Congress Catalog Number: 82-70208

Manufactured in the United States of America.

To Isabel, and to numerous friends and acquaintances who have asked me why I fly and have never really received an answer.

Contents

Introduction

Milton Brener has written the book that all pilots wish they had written. If you are still a groundling, hoping to be a pilot someday, Brener's book is both a pathway and an inspiration. If you are an old grey pelican with more than a few thousand hours flying time under your wings, you will chuckle and reminisce as you read, knowing the learning hurdles and near disasters he is about to describe. You may also find yourself learning a few new tricks about the ways that Brener has become an "old, not bold" pilot. (You know the old saying: "There are old pilots, and bold pilots, but there are no old bold pilots.")

Nearly all of us who write our flying memoirs tend to become silk-scarfed aces and romanticize the junky planes we flew, the times we were lost, the Federal Air Regulations that we, if not broke, did bend to the limits. We get carried off into wind in the wires, and sun glinting on the taut fabric, and how we belched our way out of the belly of that mean ole thunderstorm and lived to come brag about it here in the coffee room.

Brener has a rare knack among aviation writers; he is neither rip-roaring romanticist, nor teacher at the head of a snoozing classroom. I can't think of any other aviation writer, myself included, who has managed to write flying with such balance. I would bet real money that he flies just like he writes.

If you are an old head, you'll close this book thinking, I'd like to know this guy. I'd fly with him anywhere. Brener is not a professional pilot. Flying is only his avocation, albeit a dear one. But how many pilots could tell a personal narrative of something that means as much as flying does to Milt, and avoid even the slightest side-bar excursion into self-aggrandizement?

If you are a new-start, our friend Milton Brener will neither turn you away from the actual experience as being a pursuit for madmen only, nor will he drag you along with dull, pedantic writing.

His story begins with his return to aviation as a young attorney. Viewing the old airport where he recalls boyhood memories of barnstorming's golden age, he watches the shrieking jets and worries that he's too late. But there, on the other side of the airport, preserved with almost museumlike detail, are the small airplanes and the almost exclusive band of brothers gathered round the battered coffee table where the conversation is still wind, wings, and weather. He becomes hooked on flying again—this time for good.

We progress with him through student days, rich reading for the yet uninitiated, green memories for the rest of us. You fly with him through first cross-country trips, through the more ambitious later ones, and the tug-o-war of checking wind and weather with trusting wife waiting to go. Should he try for it or not? Your palms will sweat at some places along in here.

In time Milton was doing mountain flying out to Aspen in his twin. And the rich vein that flows through this latter part of the book is some of the best commonsense reporting on mountain flying. There is also some of the very best commentary on the age-old controversy of the safety of a twin-engined airplane over a good single. I've never heard it said any better.

If I were a Certified Flight Instructor, I would insist that all my new students read and even memorize parts of this book. I'm convinced it would make them better pilots . . . old pilots.

—Gordon Baxter
Flying

The Other Side of the Airport

I

Where Time Stands Still

There was a time when most private planes took off from small fields with grass landing strips, located in the country or on the outskirts of town. Some early airports even had a hangar or two and a small terminal building. Flying, even airline flying, was at that time for daredevils, not sensible people. Kids, who aren't expected to have much sense, peered through airport fences hoping to glimpse open-cockpit, cloth-covered biplanes taking off with an exhilarating roar, or gliding silently earthward.

I know a little about such things because I was born in 1930, and in the thirties relics of the romantic infancy of flying still abounded at the New Orleans Lakefront Airport, where as a child I saw them.

My gravest apprehension in those days was that I had been born too late. From the time I could read, I read about planes and flying. What I read claimed that aviation was changing rapidly and that it was going to be a different world because of it. Flying was going to be commonplace. The future spelled doom for cloth-covered planes with closed-in cabins and old open-cockpit biplanes. Pictures of the planes of the future left me cold, and my most fervent hope was that the future wouldn't come until I grew up and had a few years to savor the world of aviation as I saw it in the thirties.

That world was supposed to disappear but it never did. Like tribes of aborigines surviving in primitive areas near modern cities, the world of the private pilot has survived. There have been some changes, some accomodations to progress, but the private pilot's world as I first saw it has remained substantially intact. Had I been able during the thirties to look forty years into the future, I'm sure I would have been pleased.

There are still some small grass-strip fields in rural areas. The planes there are not much different, fundamentally, from the ones that circled lazily overhead in the thirties. And there are more planes, survivors from those days, still flying than I ever would have thought possible. However, much of the light-plane flying by private pilots—those who fly for the joy of flight alone—is not from these small fields. There is much more of this ancient world surviving than casual observers suspect.

Hidden in some obscure corner of almost every large airport is a relic whose existence is barely visible to the jet traveler. He may get a glimpse of it while looking across the huge expanse of the airport from the glass-encased observation deck of a modernistic terminal building. It is often just a cluster of tiny one- and two-engined brightly colored planes.

On occasion, he may see one of these strange craft buzzing down one of the huge runways, lifting off in the first 15 or 20 percent of it, and almost disappearing in the haze as it crosses the far end of the airport. It may hold his fancy for a moment before he continues on his way, or it may strike him as wryly humorous—this small plane in this giant airport.

This relic is an airport within an airport, often located on the other side of the field from the main terminal, or stuck at the end of the service road behind the air-freight warehouses or airline-maintenance hangers. Wherever it may be, it will harbor no lines of passengers buying tickets nor any other similarity to an airport as the jet traveler knows it. There will be a small lounge, where a few pilots are drinking coffee and checking weather. On the wall will be the inevitable airway-radio-facility chart of the United States. Concentric circles radiate outward at 100-mile intervals from a point on the chart that designates the airport location.

The main terminal has a cocktail lounge, loudspeakers, redcaps, insurance counters, barber shops and gift shops. The office at the little one across the way has vending machines for sandwiches and Cokes, line boys, gas trucks and direct lines to the nearest FAA flight-service station to simplify the filing of flight plans.

Cabs, buses and limousines drive up a huge circular drive to the entrance of the main terminal, but only private cars or taxis usually navigate the road to that other field, which is sometimes at the end of a tortuous route to the airport's outer areas. Even many cab drivers do not know the way to the general-aviation section of some large airports. In strange cities, I have on occasion lost much time with cab drivers who knew not much more than I about the location of this other airport—or even that it existed.

In the main terminal, people of all ages, types and styles of dress sit in the plush waiting areas, restaurants and cocktail lounges, discussing the things most often talked about wherever people gather—business, politics, travel, sex, weddings. They discuss the weather in casual terms.

In the lounges and coffee shops of the "fixed-base operators," of that other airport across the way, a few men and fewer women, often dressed in grease-stained Levi's or khakis, are discussing only airplanes and flying. They argue the merits of fuel-injected versus carbureted engines; low-wing versus high-wing; single engine versus multi; fixed-pitch versus constant-speed propellers. Their discussion of the weather is not casual, it's serious.

For a number of years, I have sat in coffee shops and lounges at these little airports around the country, many preserved within the encasement of a large jetport and I have heard them debating endlessly the perennial issues. Only the accents are different.

There are thousands of these small airports, some surviving on their own in rural areas—but I have sampled enough to guess fairly accurately what life is like in the rest.

You may be sure that at any one of them, wherever it is located, small groups swap tales of flying, often largely fictional, and talk or argue over half-filled coffee cups.

There will be some younger pros who spend almost all of their time looking for any kind of flying available, at any pay, or for none. They must build their hours if they are ever to reach their goal of flying for a large corporation and ultimately finding employment with a scheduled airline. They must literally fly to survive. Pay is secondary. There will be some doctors, lawyers, businessmen and tradesmen, who are apt to be there on weekends, but seldom at any other time.

You cannot tell much by age—the flight instructors are sometimes older men with young students and sometimes very young instructors with middle-aged students. There will be members of flying clubs, those who own their own planes, and those who rent. There may be some FAA personnel spending their spare time flying or talking about flying. Some of them became interested in planes because of their jobs and some sought their jobs because of their interest in planes. There are other FAA men who have no interest in planes at all and feel that if God wanted man to fly, He would have given him wings.

They are not all of a type, nor do they gravitate to the airport for the same reason. Some love only to fly and others love planes more for the mechanical challenge they present. They love to tinker with their planes as much as to fly them. From my point of view, they are fortunate. I have no mechanical proclivity, and at this stage, I am not likely to develop any. I have never been sufficiently impressed by the wonders of modern science to make a concerted effort to understand them. I assume there is some natural explanation for them and I am not consumed with a desire to know the details.

Yet every time I see a plane break ground, I think it a miracle. I have always been fascinated by flight and anything connected with it. The sight of a distant speck identifiable as a plane aloft can still hold my attention and I can't remember a time when it did not.

As a boy of eight or nine my favorite outing was a trip to New Orleans Lakefront Airport. There I could observe these miracles of planes actually lifting into flight and gliding gently to earth. For an hour or so I could walk among them, touch the fabric, and look inside at the mysterious dials, gadgets, levers and pedals that made them work, and I hoped to get a glimpse of one of those fortunate men who passed their days flying airplanes. I used to look at every man who passed, wondering if he were one of them. But the men I saw did not look or sound like the supermen I assumed all pilots to be and I was much relieved to learn that they were not. Because I was fortunate enough to be spared contact with the ordinary mortals who actually did fly, the aura of the supernatural persisted. It was many years before I was forced to accept that those who piloted the planes were men as ordinary as those who worked in offices, sold insurance, operated buses, or ran for public office. With equal disdain, I would read and hear of honors and awards bestowed upon men for achievement in this or that field of endeavor. If they did not fly planes, what good was their money or their honors?

I saved small change from a weekly allowance or from odd jobs and subscribed to books and periodicals about planes and flying, although some of them were far beyond my ability to comprehend. The most rewarding and lasting investment was a fifteen-minute plane ride over the city in a high-wing four-seater. It cost five dollars for the fifteen minutes. I was about nine years old and I was the envy of my two friends who shared my interest. One of them accompanied me to the airport and then waited, earthbound, for my return.

He was too proud and too envious to question me beyond a simple, "How was it?" and he let me escape with an evasive, "Great." I'm glad he didn't ask more. I was afraid I would destroy his enthusiasm, which I sometimes felt was fed, at least in part, by my own; and I needed the companionship of his continued interest. In our childish imagination, the glory of flight was the exhilaration of great speed. We spoke of the anticipated thrill of watching cities and the natural features of the earth streak backward beneath our wings with such speed as to disappear in a blur.

How could I have explained that at several thousand feet above the city we hovered motionless; that far from streaking backward, the buildings and roadways of New Orleans stood almost stationary beneath us; that I had no sensation of motion at all.

Nor could I have explained to him the thrill of looking down on the city and seeing one's whole world compressed to the size of a picture, a picture at once familiar yet foreign. Never could I have explained the exhilaration of seeing in one glance places that were ordinarily worlds apart. From the air the distance between our neighborhood and downtown New Orleans, or even Lake Pontchartrain, took up but a small portion of my field of vision. Within this elaborate toy city that lay at our feet was the most intricate detail. I could look to the east and in the distance see enticing hints of the Mississippi Gulf Coast, a popular resort area, a three-hour car ride at that time.

It didn't require much imagination to realize that more altitude would bring into focus the long stretch of white beach on the other side of the state line and perhaps even recognizable hotels and beach houses.

But none of that would have mattered as much to my friend as the fact that there was no motion. Speed was what held our fascination and speed was what earned our continued interest and dedication. It was for the thrill of speed that we made so many plans and talked endlessly of the future. So I reported to him in the vaguest generalities about my first flight and left it to him to find out the specifics for himself, as he inevitably would.

The plans for our future were quite elaborate. There were three of us, and we planned to spend adulthood flying the globe. We were going to do it in formation, in three single-engine, single-seater airplanes. We gave not the slightest thought to how we would afford the maintenance and gas, let alone the purchase price of our machines. Nor did we consider such practical matters as earning a livelihood. The prospect of permanent ties—marriage and children—never entered our thoughts. All that mattered was that we would learn to fly in the Army Air Corps and that after our tour of duty we would be committed to an endless search for adventure.

We prepared for our careers by buying every periodical we could afford on the subject of flying, and by riding our bikes in formation around the city, just as we planned to fly our planes.

From time to time, I still wonder about my two companions. Undoubtedly, they went on to learn a profession or a trade, and to earn a living without a backward glance. They indulged, probably, not even a casual reminiscence about our impossible plans. I am sure that they matured, grew to manhood and put away childish things. If by chance their love for flying persisted, it was no doubt channeled constructively and led to a career as an airline or corporate pilot, or other well-paid professional. But I doubt that. I am certain that for them flying was a childish dream that went the way that most of them do when children grow up. They probably got over it.

I never did. There were two more short flights: one in a DC-3 as a result of winning some contest, the details of which I have long forgotten, and another in a fabric-covered tandem two-seater, probably a Piper Cub. My only concession to practicality, at least by my first year of high school, was a willingness to make a career as an airline pilot, rather than as a lone ace flying the world in search of adventure. Even that comparatively mundane ambition earned a quiet sneer from my high school counselor. It was no future for a bright young boy.

But he gets none of the blame. If I really wanted to be an airline pilot, I support I could have been one, or at least I could have tried. Somewhere I took a wrong turn.

In partial defense, I must say that a career in aviation was not easy to come by in the days following my graduation from high school. The market for pilots was glutted by tens of thousands of returning World War II veterans. It sometimes seemed that almost everyone knew how to fly and there were many pilots with combat-sharpened experience who went jobless. Five-thousand-hour veterans sold insurance, encyclopedias, or automobiles, and waited to hear from airlines. And the airlines sifted the applications slowly, accepting only one of each several hundred, even in those days of expanding postwar airline operations.

I sometimes felt, as I looked upon the sorry scene, that my private world had been taken over by an army of occupation. In the prewar days of the thirties, no one thought of a career in flying. On the rare occasions when I heard of someone who flew, or wanted to, I felt an immediate kinship. I probably felt as one with a rare blood type who happens on another of the same rare type. In those days no man who flew did so because of money, prestige, pleasant working conditions, or convenience. He flew, or wanted to fly, I assumed, because he loved it.

I entered college in 1946, the year after the war ended. Enrollment was swollen with returning veterans. Some had been fliers, but very few had wanted to fly. To some it had offered the least gruesome of the alternatives available. Some had been smitten by the wartime glorification of the "wild blue." Some were bitter. Some said they never wanted to set foot in a plane again. Some were looking for jobs flying airplanes because, as they admitted, it was all they knew how to do.

It seemed that the world of aviation would never be the same again. Perhaps it never has, but the degree and extent of the change was grossly misjudged and exaggerated by the industry, and particularly by overenthusiastic investors. The aviation magazines were filled with articles and advertisements heralding a new age in which every returning flier would settle for nothing less than his own plane. Soon, the stories went, planes would take the place of cars, at least for intercity travel. They would be mass-produced and every family would have one. Flying schools proliferated. "Learn to fly," read the ads. "It's as easy as learning to drive a car."

It never happened. Flying a plane is not like driving a car. It really is not quite as easy, nor, except upon taking the most intricate precautions, quite as safe—nor a fraction as cheap.

The profusion of family fliers never came. Families did not fly airplanes; they kept on driving cars. A boom in aviation came, but it belonged to the air carriers and it reached fruition with the arrival of the jets in the sixties. The light plane never did take its place with the second car, the TV, or the stereo in the litany of every middle-class family's necessities. Today, as in the thirties, most people will not set foot in a light plane. The predicted traffic jams in the air never materialized.

I read the ads and I believed them. For a while I accepted and even anticipated the "tomorrow" that they promised, as practical considerations preempted all serious thoughts of a career in aviation. The expense of training was prohibitive and in value no match for the experience of the veteran.

I attended Tulane University, in New Orleans, and floundered in one pursuit after another until I settled, ultimately, into the serious study of law. But even after graduating from law school, at the age of twenty-two, the bug was still there. This was 1952 and the Korean War raged; for how long it would continue, no one seemed able to guess. Military service was a certainty for almost everyone. Mine had been postponed by attendance at college, but would undoubtedly not be postponed much longer. The lure of Air Force flight training was strong, but once again I succumbed to practical considerations. Too much had been invested by now in the study of law.

I probably would have done the same under any circumstances, but the decision was made just a little easier by the fact that the Air Force was now jet-propelled. These were not the planes that captured my imagination as a boy and the lure of flight at the speed of sound at 30,000 feet and above was not irresistible. The Air Force clinched it by refusing to waive a prohibition against married aviation cadets. I was engaged to be married.

So I served in the Judge Advocate General's Corps of the Army, spending ten months in Korea and a year in Okinawa. Much of the time in Korea was spent traveling that primitive, dusty country in light planes of 200 hp or less, at speeds of no more than 150 miles per hour and at altitudes not much higher than the 4,000-foot mountain ridges. The shooting had ended eight months before I arrived. Often we flew the valleys considerably below the higher peaks on either side of us. Those flights erased every suspicion that whatever appeal flying may have had for me might have been a passing fancy.

I was discharged from the service in September, 1956. One Sunday afternoon in May, 1957, I went to the New Orleans Lakefront Airport. It was the first time I had been there in five years. The "feel" of the airport was now more similar to that of the earlier days than to the bustling airport it was in the forties, swollen as it seemed then with military activities.

Gone also were all signs of scheduled airline activity. The Lakefront Airport had been the only airport serving New Orleans during the thirties and until the end of World War II. During that epoch, all domestic airlines flew the legendary two-engine, twenty-one-passenger Douglas DC-3. As a boy I used to look at those leviathans and marvel that so much metal could take to the skies so gracefully. I could not imagine that the "3" would ever be improved upon or replaced. I assumed that it represented the ultimate in transport by air. After the war, however, these slender beauties were dwarfed by the more powerful

DC-4s and the four-engine DC-6s. These were too much airplane for Lakefront Airport. A new field, Moisant International, was constructed about ten miles west of the city to accomodate the airlines. Lakefront Airport now belonged to the military and to "general aviation," a term loosely used to describe all flying other than airline and military.

That day in 1957, when I went to see about flight training, I was looking only for the least-expensive school. I intended to wander into any one of the fixed-base operations that lined the field on either side of the main terminal building. These were the small one- and two-man operations that in the prewar days rented fabric-covered, single-engine, 90 mph, two-seater Luscombes, Taylorcrafts, Aeroncas, and Piper Cubs. They furnished tie-down or hangar space and maintenance to those who owned and kept their aircraft at the airport. They furnished gas, oil, maintenance, and overnight service to itinerant aircraft. They gave flying lessons for about ten or twelve dollars per hour.

Except for the signs that proclaimed that the flying schools were "V.A. Approved," I found that the place really hadn't changed very much.

II

Forces in Balance

I was twenty-seven when I first handled the controls of an airplane and flying was no longer an exotic adventure either for me or for the world in general. By the late fifties a whole generation had been on intimate terms with aviation. Airline travel was no longer a luxury for the wealthy or a challenge for the adventurous. In the thirties, the older generation frowned on my professed desire to fly as foolhardy; in the fifties, they dismissed it as merely pointless. In the thirties, the drone of a plane overhead drew many upward stares, but twenty years later, the more powerful drones drew attention from very few.

But I was one of the few. By now I was satisfied that my fascination with flight, not having subsided at this stage, was not going to evaporate with time.

My first venture into flying lasted a little over three years before, one day in 1960, the press of other matters caused me to put it on the shelf for another day. I had accumulated about 130 hours flying time, an average of less than one hour per week. The experience I acquired during those three years was in some ways limited, but in other ways more valuable than the numbers suggest. Though the planes were simpler than those I flew in later years and required less skill in pushing levers and gadgets, they demanded more in the basics of airmanship.

None of them had retractable gear or a constant-speed propeller, which is a more efficient blade than the fixed-pitch prop on the older planes. All of them were high-wing craft with "conventional gear," that is, with a tail wheel instead of a nose wheel. "Taildraggers," they're called. Landing the taildragger is significantly harder, but much more satisfying when done correctly than a plane with tricycle gear, that is, with a nose wheel.

With the exceptions of two all-metal Luscombes, all these planes were cloth-covered. With the exception of a 145 hp four-seater Stinson Voyager, which was several notches more advanced than the others, they were side-by-side two-seaters. Except for the Stinson, they had no flaps (a movable portion of the rear inboard part of the wing, designed to permit a steeper descent without excessive increase in speed) nor any electrical system. The prop had to be started by hand. Except for the 120 mph Stinson, these planes rarely indicated over 100 mph, except in a dive.

Even in the late fifties these birds looked like they had long stories to tell. They were not as sleek—or "clean," as pilots say—or otherwise as impressive as the new tricycle-geared Cessnas operated by other schools on the field.

My first flight was in a 65 hp Taylorcraft, which is more a sailplane with an engine than an airplane. When you cut the power on a "T" craft, it sometimes seemed as though it didn't make any difference and that it would just float forever. This was especially true on a summer afternoon, when you could literally see the heat rising off the asphalt runway.

The school had two of these "T" craft and another 65 hp plane known as an Aeronca Chief. The Chief had a big, drooping belly and looked as if it would soon give birth to a little Aeronca Chief. It was even slower than the "T" craft, going only about 85 mph, as I recall. Even the birds seemed to recognize how gentle the plane was, or perhaps they assumed that any bird with as big a belly as the Aeronca could not be very dangerous. I recall on one short cross-country trip birds soaring and gliding along, often level with the Chief at 2,500 feet, and my concern that I would tangle with one or perhaps a flock of them. The brazen creatures seemed to be eyeing me with curiosity as I passed them and weren't the slightest bit inclined to get out of my way.

For me the biggest attraction of the Luscombes was the fact that they had a "stick"—a bar protruding vertically from the floor—to control the lateral and horizontal attitude of the plane, rather than the automobile-type wheel of the others. Control is available by a flick of the wrist, a simpler, more natural movement, and I have often wondered why more light planes, especially trainers, do not have them.

Finally, there was the four-place, 145 hp, 120 mph Stinson Voyager—a "real airplane"—that is, one designed to travel from one place to another, one that had four comfortable seats and a roomy cabin. It was one that you could take on a trip of several hundred miles and not get passed up by a diesel truck on the highway, as I did once in the Chief while battling a modest headwind.

In the late fifties these were merely old airplanes. Today they are regarded as near-antiques and pilots speak of them with respect if not exactly with veneration.

Admittedly, there were times when I felt almost self-conscious in these tarnished, aged craft, and had a yen to learn in one of the modern tri-geared trainers with eye-catching paint schemes and fancier instrument panels. It was usually those planes whose pictures adorned the flying magazines. They were the ones depicted at rest in exotic places and surrounded by beautiful people with cheery smiles, or flying into a Caribbean sunset or a Colorado sunrise. It must have been visions evoked by such ads that made me feel like a poor relation in the grease-stained, patched-up, decrepit-looking contraptions in which I earned my private license.

But these planes came cheaper. Although I was learning to fly on the G.I. Bill, with the government paying 75 percent of the costs, the other 25 percent was no small matter.

My instructor for the first few flights was the first of several I had during those three years. He was also one of the finest I have come across during that time, or since. He was cool, composed, and completely at home in an airplane, the result of several thousand hours of flying four-engine bombers across the Atlantic during World War II. He was now a senior engineering student at Tulane University and taught flying part time. Several months after I started, he graduated, took a job elsewhere, and moved away.

He actually matched the imaginary ideal of the flier I had conjured as a boy. But of course I was not a child and should have known that he would not be typical. I have since flown with many instructors, a greater number than would be ideal for efficient learning, and I have met others. Most have been good ones. But there have been some, I am convinced, who did not really like flying, and a few who were really afraid of it. There have been others who obviously did not like people and at least several who, in my belief, hated or feared both people and planes. But fortunately my first instructor had a temperament well suited to teaching and was as much at ease with people as with airplanes. He was quiet, but did not need to talk to convey his love of flying.

Flying came no easier to me than to most who have always had solid ground under their feet. When I first gripped the controls (and that, literally, is what I did), I found that the horizon was erratic and disobedient. It did not have any natural inclination to stay where it belonged, as it did when I was on solid ground. It crept upward along the windshield as the noise of the engine and the wind whistling past the leaky "T" craft increased, both in volume and in pitch. It dropped below the nose as the noise level lessened and the engine labored. It turned slantwise and made crazy angles along the windshield. The horizon seemed to have no built-in stability. It swung like a pendulum. It rocked back and forth like a rocking chair that would not quit.

At some point during that first session, perhaps earlier than it now seems, the horizon appeared to tire of its odd motions about the same time I tired of fighting the controls. The following week, both the horizon and I renewed our game of tag, but we both settled down substantially quicker. I soon realized I was moving over the familiar ground east of New Orleans in more or less level flight and was, in a manner of speaking, flying the airplane. If I had not mastered flying, I had at least come to grips with the basics of straight and level flight. I had learned what I had always been told, what I read and believed, but did not fully understand. Almost all planes certified by the FAA want to fly straight and level and will do so with only the slightest coaxing. They almost fly themselves.

They do not literally fly themselves, as is often claimed, and if left to their own devices (depending on the setting of the trim tabs on control surfaces, power setting, smoothness of the air, and other factors), will go into a spiral, or a series of roller-coaster climbs and dives. But they do so very slowly, at least for a while, and with only the gentlest nudging fly straight and level as they are designed to do. This had been merely my first of several bouts with one of the most tenacious enemies of every aspect of the airman's art—overcontrol.

I went through a succession of instructors and planes as I became more and more acclimated to a three-dimensional medium. If the anticipated transitory thrill was missing, its place was taken by discoveries of more lasting value. Flight is a study in symmetry, a kaleidoscope of changing relationships between opposing forces. It becomes apparent even in the simple maneuver known as turns.

In straight and level flight, it is the pilot's purpose to keep the world right side up. To turn, you must deliberately tilt the earth over on its side. This is hard for a ground animal to accept, but there is no other way. A plane turns by banking. The lift that sustains flights acts perpendicularly to the wings. When the wings are banked, and no longer level with the horizon, the lifting force remains perpendicular to the wings, not to the earth, and it literally lifts the plane around a curved path or turn in the direction in which it is banked.

The steeper the bank, the sharper the turn. Except through a skillful (or reckless) manipulation of controls that forces the plane into gyrations for which it was not designed, the plane cannot bank without turning and it cannot turn without banking.

The two-dimensional creature does not feel comfortable with this. When the plane banks, he does not sit upright in his seat; he leans, consciously or otherwise, against the turn. This behavior can been seen in practically every new student or passenger in small planes. Turn right and he leans to the left, trying to minimize his angle to the earth, trying to stay familiarly perpendicular to it. But it is not necessary. In a properly executed turn, centrifugal force, the force that tends to propel you in your original direction, will overcome any tendency to slide to the inside of the turn. Shut your eyes in a properly coordinated turn and you cannot tell the direction of turn. Nor can you tell whether the forces that press you firmly into your seat result from a turn or an increase in speed.

These forces, which also make you weigh more, and also cause the blood to rush to your head, are known as G forces. They result from acceleration, and acceleration, according to the physicists, is a change in speed or direction. Shut your eyes in a plane and you cannot tell a change in speed from a change in direction.

As the steepness of the plane's bank and the sharpness of its turn increase, the G forces increase at a far greater rate. During gentle turns, the only kind performed by airliners, the increase in G forces is rarely noticed and never uncomfortable. Beyond 30 degrees, G forces increase sharply and beyond 60 degrees dramatically.

Not only the pilot and passengers but also the entire airplane weigh more in a turn, so as the plane loads up with G forces, it starts to lose altitude. And, because the engineers have seen to it that the nose will point in the direction in which the plane moves, the nose tends to drop and speed increases. These characteristics of a turning airplane, improperly understood by the early pilots, were the undoing of many of them when they first flew into clouds. But that is another story.

For the student pilot who limits his practice to clear skies, these forces are not dangerous, merely challenging.

Then follows a further explanation of the complexities of the laws of aerodynamics in the form of climbs, descents, and airspeed control. They go together. The speed of the plane is closely related to its vertical movement and they are both related to power control. You cannot change any one—power, speed, or rate of climb or descent—without affecting at least one of the other two, or both of them. At a fixed power setting you cannot change speed without changing the rate or direction of vertical movement. Descend from level flight at the same power setting and speed increases; climb and it decreases. In level flight, reduce power but maintain the same speed and you descend. Increase power, maintain the same speed and you climb.

Flight is a complex world of intricate relationships where the simplest maneuvers defy simple explanation. The exact mechanics and the underlying aerodynamic theory of the simplest elements of flight are still, seventy-eight years after the Wright brothers, the subject of serious debate. It is legitimately presumed by most students that the fundamentals are governed by immutable rules that are not subject to controversy. And it is difficult and disheartening for them to hear that even the most learned in the field do not agree as to what control governs the rate of climb or descent and which control governs airspeed, but they don't. They argue, and not only over empty coffee cups and cold sandwiches, but in magazine articles, technical publications, lectures, and books.

Does power control airspeed and do elevators, those movable portions of the horizontal tail surface, control climb and descent? Or is it the other way around? Only within the last few years, after seventy-eight years of heavier-than-air flight, has the official FAA–approved method of instruction on this fundamental subject been significantly changed.

It all stems from the fact that planes are necessarily built to be stable for whatever "angle of attack" the plane is trimmed.

The angle of attack is the angle at which the wind meets the wing. The plane never flies precisely in the same vertical direction in which the wing is pointed. The air always strikes the underside of the wing at some angle, very slight at high speeds, greater at lower speeds. At low speeds, even when holding a constant altitude, the plane flies with its nose high. It is this angle of attack that gives the plane its lift and sustains flight.

As long as the plane's weight is constant and it is not weighted down with increasing G forces as it is in a turn, the speed is governed entirely by this angle of attack.

With high power, a low-angle attack and, consequently, high speed, can be maintained at a constant altitude. With reduced power, the same speed can be maintained only with the same angle of attack, which means nose down, the direction in which the plane automatically moves when the power is reduced.

This tendency of the nose to drop when power is reduced and thereby to maintain constant speed has been carefully engineered into the plane for good reasons. If it were not, the plane would be very tricky and dangerous to fly since it is airspeed that keeps the plane flying.

Thus, only by the use of the elevator control can airspeed be altered, say many knowledgeable pilots and authorities in aerodynamics. But, say others, when power is reduced, the only reason the nose dropped in the first place was because the plane initially tended to slow. So power really controls speed.

The problem is that when things happen simultaneously it is difficult to say what causes what. Supporters of both sides agree only that use of elevator and throttle together, when coordinated, control both an altitude change and speed. As to which control is primary for which change in condition, speed on the one hand, or climb and descent on the other, the arguments continue among those who are interested.

None of which means anything, however, to many of the old pros who fly for a living. Many superb pilots know little about such things and could care less. They just fly. And they do what they do because that is what they have to do to make the plane do what they want it to. Many of them do beautiful things with airplanes. Their execution of simple maneuvers—take-offs, climbs, turns, and landings—is a matter of flawless precision. Remarkably so, with some of them, are their loops, barrel rolls and Cuban eights. They cannot tell you what they do or why, any more than they can be expected to explain the mechanics behind the simple motion known as walking.

I remember asking one of these vets a specific question about executing wheel landings in a big bear of an airplane known as a Twin Beech. This is a twin-engine taildragger that has to be landed by being flown onto the ground with power, touching down on the main wheels first. I was having the devil's own time with it. I asked this grizzled pro, who had logged almost 2,000 hours in these Twin Beeches alone, something about the elevator control during landing. I asked about whether he applied forward pressure on the yoke before touching down, or after touching down; I don't remember exactly what.

I only remember the blank look on his face as he looked far

away and unconsciously moved his left hand as though it were on the yoke and his right hand as though gripping a pair of throttles. He moved his hands almost imperceptibly as he mentally brought his huge workhorse of a plane over the fence and flared to a landing.

Then he told me he didn't know, but he said he would try to remember to notice what he did the next time he flew one and that he would be sure to tell me.

Such oblivion about the mechanics and the aerodynamics of flight is not only understandable, but quite natural to those for whom flight is the particular form of tedium by which they earn a living. In an instructor, it is less understandable, though almost as prevalent. The approach to the subject is disarmingly simple. When you reduce power, the nose drops because it does—that's the way the plane flies. When you add power, the nose comes up, so you don't gain any speed. To gain speed you have to trim the yoke forward as you add power. The reason is simple: That is the way the plane is built.

The attitude is contagious and seems quite natural. It's the way things are, like a straight line's being the shortest distance between two points, and I was quite content to learn to fly by feel.

And sooner or later you do come to get the feel of flying, or of its particular aspects. You learn when it feels right on takeoff roll, when it is ready to lift off, and when it is climbing most efficiently. It becomes second nature to hold right rudder in a climb to prevent the nose from yawing to the left.

The nose always wants to yaw to the left in a climb. You accept the instructor's explanation that yawing to the left is caused by something called "torque." Since the propeller turns to the right, the plane tends to turn left; this is because for every action there is an equal but opposite reaction. What instructors don't always explain is why such a rotating reaction would be countered with rudders rather than with ailerons, considering that it's the ailerons that are used to roll a plane or to prevent it from rolling. You leave it till later to learn that torque is merely the simplest to explain, but the least important of the forces contributing to the left-turning, or left-yawing, tendency of the plane at high-power/low-speed configurations such as the climb. Sooner or later it becomes second nature to hold right rudder as the plane accelerates and climbs and you think no more about it.

You go through the same process with all of it. You practice them until they feel right. You learn to stall and to recover without really knowing why a stall happens. You are told and you accept that the plane stalls because of an excessive angle of attack.

To execute a stall is simple—you cut the power and hold the nose up. The nose want to drop when you cut power, but you hold it up. It gets heavier, so you exert more pressure to keep it up. The nose is high, but the plane is not climbing, and may even be sinking. The nose strains against you now. The prop slows, a warning horn blows. The angle of attack is now such that the underside of the wing is blocking the smooth flow of air over the wing's top. The plane shudders, trying to tell you something.

What it is trying to tell you is that planes were not meant to fly at such high angles of attack. Suddenly it drops. The plane is no longer flying. The nose falls slightly below the horizon, though the angle is not so steep as the path of the falling plane itself. Only when back pressure is released will the nose drop sufficiently to regain flying speed. Only when the wings point in the general direction in which the plane is moving—which is quite steep—will the airspeed build. Only then can you resume level flight. You practice stalling until it becomes so natural a thing that explanations seem superfluous.

The characteristics of the plane as it approaches to land become just as natural. The approach is with power off, or greatly reduced. The landing is simply a stall, or the approach to a stall, executed a few inches off the ground rather than at several thousand feet, where stalls are first taught. But before the approach to landings feels natural, it feels unnatural. There is a lot of "unlearning" to do.

On the first few tries, you see that you're coming in short, so you do the "natural" thing. You bring the controls back to hold the nose higher so it will point farther off, namely at the touchdown point on the runway, rather than at the houses across the street from the airport where it is pointed now. For a moment it works—the nose rises and remains pointed at the edge of the runway.

Soon, however, you notice that the nose is pointed once again at the houses and that you are descending faster than before. Leave the controls as they are and both the airport and the houses will soon rise farther in your windshield, and your nose will point now at the shopping center or filling station on the near side of the houses.

Come back harder on the stick, and you sink faster. You do not lengthen your glide that way—you shorten it. Continue the process and sooner or later you will land short. Perhaps you will stall. But the instructor will not sit silent forever. He will tell you what will some day become second nature. He will tell you that you must maintain a certain minimum speed on the approach. You can slow your descent, your rate of sink, by back pressure only until you slow to that speed. If the plane slows below that speed, the rate of sink will increase. The more back pressure from that point on, the more the rate of sink will increase.

This is one situation in which you must control altitude with power and airspeed with the elevators. There are no two opinions. You leave for another day very interesting texts on maximum lift-to-drag ratio and the back side of the power curve, which explain questions that tantalize through months of instruction.

The most difficult of elementary maneuvers is the landing. It doesn't come at once to anyone. The student must find the ground and he must find it himself. The art of touching down is a skill like walking that comes with practice but cannot really be taught. The student may flare, level over the runway too high, stall too high off the ground, and drop it in with a bang that startles him, and sometimes the instructor. Then he will compensate by flaring too low and allow the plane to touch with excessive speed. Then it will balloon up a few feet and perhaps bounce several times before staying down for good.

Sometimes, when he comes in too fast, he will succeed in

holding the plane off the runway to lose flying speed and thereby avoid bouncing. But then he will sail down the runway and eat up half or more of it before bleeding off the excess speed. This is a dangerous habit on short fields. Next time, of course, he will overcompensate, come in too slowly, and when he flares, the plane will drop out from under him.

Most students require twelve to sixteen hours of dual instruction before soloing, and half of that time or more is spent learning to land. Progress is often slow. A bad landing often fires an angry compulsion to correct the mistake, but the process cannot be hurried. A landing must be followed by a takeoff and climb to at least a "traffic-pattern" altitude, which is 800 feet at most airports. The student must then fly this traffic pattern, a rectangular pattern to the left of the active runway before returning for another landing.

He climbs after takeoff to 300 or 400 feet, turns left 90 degrees, flies the crosswind leg a few hundred yards or so, and turns 90 degrees left again to fly the downwind leg while continuing the climb to 800 feet. During this downwind leg, he flies parallel to the active runway but in the direction opposite from the approach path for landing.

Opposite to the approach end of the runway, he reduces power to start the descent and turns left 90 degrees again for the "base leg" of the pattern. He is now 90 degrees from the final approach course to the runway and descending. One more 90-degree turn and he is on "final" at an altitude of anywhere from 300 to 500 feet. He keeps the touchdown point at the same spot in his windshield. If it drops, he reduces power, or throttles back completely. If it rises, he adds power. The airspeed is controlled with the elevators—at 65 to 75 mph in most small trainers.

He flares over the runway—power off. As the plane settles, he holds it off by increasing back pressure, but not so much that it balloons. He waits to hear the gentle squeak of rubber on asphalt but the plane settles faster, and there's still no runway. He decides he'd better add power to slow the descent.

Too late. The plane smacks into the asphalt with a sickening thud and bounces. How can any plane take such a beating? The instructor—depending on his experience, temperament, and mood—shouts angrily, or calmly explains that the student misjudged his height by staring at one point ahead. He tells the student he must get perspective by allowing his eyes to dart to various points, front and side. Or he laughs and makes a funny remark. Or he says nothing except, maybe, "Take it around again."

They're called, appropriately, "touch and goes." Each circuit takes about four minutes, sometimes more. In a one-hour session, allowing time for taxiing and engine runup, the student can make eight or ten landings, at most. It can be fatiguing, and there is a point of diminishing returns.

It can also be frustrating. Four minutes of flying, perhaps perfectly executed except for one sloppy landing, blown in a matter of seconds. Four or five minutes before it can be corrected on a second try. The student rarely makes the same mistake twice in succession. Too high one time, too low the next. Too fast one time, too slow the next.

Some students learn gradually but consistently. Their progress is steady. They are the exceptions. Most students reach plateaus, seemingly endless periods of no progress, punctuated by short, rapid periods of improvement. For most weekend pilots, the frustration is compounded by the long intervals between lessons. Two steps forward, one step backward; then two steps forward, two steps backward. At this stage once a week is barely enough, but until a certain minimum proficiency is achieved, even an accelerated schedule is unavailing.

One day it all comes together—everything clicks. Something has happened inside, which has nothing to do with conscious effort. The student has found the runway. He has the feel of the landing. The instructor may voice approval or say nothing. But one day, as the student taxis back to the parking area, he hears that the instructor is getting out of the plane but that the student is staying in and making one, two, or three circuits around the traffic pattern by himself.

Much has been written and said about the first solo. It is often marked by handshaking and ceremony. On the occasion of my own first solo, I expected I was undertaking what would become a memorable moment in my flying career.

But I did nothing that first time around the pattern alone that I had not done many times before. The only difference was the absence of the instructor. Minus his 200 or so pounds, the plane climbed more quickly and floated longer, but slower, with the engine throttled back. Otherwise, it was simply more relaxing and enjoyable without someone to point out my every little shortcoming or imperfection in technique.

Flying has brought some memorable moments, but neither at the time, nor since, have those first three solo circuits around the field ever seemed to me more than just another step in the whole process. I waited in vain for that swell of pride and feeling of freedom I had been promised. In the instructing I have done, I have tried to minimize the importance of the first solo flight because students tend to attach so much importance to it. I see no reason to solo a student at the first moment it can be accomplished safely, and no reason to lead him to believe he has reached a milestone. If he continues to fly, there will be milestones enough.

For me, the most significant aspect of my first solo was the knowledge that I would soon leave the airport traffic pattern and ultimately the practice area near the airport and take a look at something beyond that ten-mile radius. Learning the basics had been interesting, but I had always looked at flying as a means of exploring, and the scenery beneath the practice area east of New Orleans gets old fast.

III

Time and Distance

I have taken in recent years a number of relatively long flights alone—flights of from 1,000 to 2,000 miles—but I was never so much alone as I was during my first few cross-country trips in the late fifties. The longest of these was no more than 200 miles.

That I was a novice was one of the less-important factors contributing to my general feeling of isolation. The most important factor was the absence of a little black box known as a radio. Pilots refer to their radio as a "navcom," "nav" for navigation, "com" for communication. One black box controls both. You set up the communication frequency on one side of the box and the navigation frequency on the other. The planes I flew in the late fifties had no com and no nav. They never even had an electrical system. In a flight across open country from one town to another it isn't the communication aspect of the radio that breaks the loneliness as much as it is the navigation part.

It may be nice to hear a human voice wafting into the cabin from some unseen location on the ground and to realize that someone knows you're up there, but there isn't really much he can tell you other than weather information, which probably isn't accurate anyway. If you're talking to an air-traffic controller who is looking at a radar screen, he can tell you where you are in case you don't know, and he can tell you of any areas of thunderstorm or rain shower activity along your flight path. But most amateur pilots who are not rated to fly instruments, as I was not in the fifties, talk only to flight service stations. The man at the flight service station has no idea where you are unless *you* tell *him,* and the weather information he has is spotty and it may be an hour old.

The offices of flight service stations have teletype machines, over which they receive weather observations taken each hour from various stations in the vicinity. The observations include such things as amount of cloud cover, height of clouds, visibility, surface wind velocity and direction, and temperature and dew point (meaning the temperature at which the air will be saturated and below which temperature fog will form).

This is all very helpful, but it doesn't tell you much about the weather between stations and it doesn't tell you what has happened since the last summary, or sequence report, as it is called. Flight service stations also receive official forecasts over the teletype, which are just as likely to be wrong as right. What most flight service stations lack are windows. The man in the flight service station cannot look outside and tell you what the weather is doing at his own station. He can only tell you what's on the teletype, and pilots have even been known to receive reports of clear skies and a rosy forecast in the midst of a torrential downpour.

No, the biggest loss is not the voice; it is a little needle that centers when you are on course and slides to the right if you drift to the left of course and to the left if you drift to the right. It is called a VOR, which is short for "very high frequency omni range," known usually as the "omni." To the nonpilot, it is an apparently silent piece of electronic gadgetry with a needle that swings right or left. To the pilot, it shouts, "You are drifting to the right" or, "You are being blown rapidly to the left of course." Or it soothingly reassures him: "You are on course and holding nicely."

Practically all air navigation over land today is guided by omni stations—several thousand of them in the United States alone. You track according to them, but along a path that you, as pilot, select. You track away from them in whatever direction you choose, and whether you stay on your selected path or drift from it—as a result of crosswind or inattention—is told to you by the all-knowing needle.

I have seen the omni stations, those little white cones, all over the country, at airports, on mountaintops, or in open fields. The VHF frequencies on which they operate are limited to line of sight. They do not follow the curve of the earth, and if the omni station is over the horizon, you cannot receive it. The higher your altitude, the greater the distance from which you can pick up the signal. You track outbound from one station until you're halfway to the next, then inbound to that one. Usually, you will track to stations about 20 miles apart in the northeastern part of the country, where omnis, like everything else, are more plentiful; to maybe fifty or sixty miles in parts of the West, where the omnis, like the towns and the people, are sparse.

In good weather, as you approach the station, you can spot the small white cone, and a service road connecting it to the main road or highway. In bad weather you can't see them, but you can visualize one beneath you as you see the needle quiver and a little arrow suddenly switch from "to" to "from," indicating that you've passed the station and that on the bearing you have selected you are no longer going to the station, but are traveling from it.

Omni stations will disappear one day. They will go the way of the bonfires that used to light the hillsides to guide the mail-planes or the giant searchlights that illuminated the sky for commercial flights in the twenties and thirties. In those days planes flew from one beacon to the next, much as the planes of today track from one omni to another.

There are already in limited operation new systems of navigation that will make these omni stations obsolete. The white cones will be relics. There is in operation a VLF (a very low frequency) system that will not be limited to line of sight, nor subject to the unpredictability and inaccuracies of the low-frequency beacons that preceded the omni. Several such VLF stations strategically located around the world will suffice for all air navigation.

There is talk of seven satellites, performing essentially the same function, and talk of a global navigation system. Already, ocean-crossing commercial flights carry multiple inertial navigation systems (INS). These are remarkable computer systems, operating with gyros, which permit precise navigation from any point on the earth's surface to any other point via an arc of the great circle. This INS navigation is without any ground facility at all; it is entirely self-contained. Every radio facility on the earth, or in satellites above it, could go out of commission at once and still this miraculous gadget would guide the pilot straight to the airport of his destination. The cost of these items is about $150,000. They are not only too expensive but at present too heavy for light planes—but there is always tomorrow.

The purpose of all of these marvelous navigational gadgets is to do accurately and quickly the computations that were largely guesswork for the oldtimers, who had nothing for navigation but a compass and a clock. Time and distance, they called it. You draw a line on a map from your airport of departure to your airport of destination. You figure the course by the angle of the line to the nearest meridian of longitude, which runs from the "true" North Pole to the "true" South Pole, the points about which the earth rotates. The compass you use, however, doesn't point to true north—it points to magnetic north, a point somewhere to the side of true north. The magnetic north pole is, of course, south of the North Pole, as is everything on earth. The exact location of magnetic north varies from time to time, so you have to add or subtract a few degrees, as much as 23 degrees in some parts of the world, to correct for this variation.

The metal inside the airplane causes its own problems and there may be one, two, or three degrees of deviation to be added or subtracted in order to know what heading to hold on your compass. Then, you simply measure your distance, figure out your airspeed, and rely on the clock to tell you when you have arrived.

All of this is tedious, but it is scientific and it is predictable. It can be done, and except for one additional factor, a pilot could theoretically navigate with this method almost as accurately and as reliably through a solid overcast as one could by using the most sophisticated electronics. That factor is the wind.

Before we take a look at the impossible mess that the unpredictable winds make of time-and-distance navigation when there is no visual contact with the ground, let us admit that flying by compass and clock alone, without reference to the ground, would not justify a feeling of security even in a dead calm.

Let us imagine such a flight. There is no wind, but you are in dense clouds, or visibility is so low that you cannot see the ground, at least not well enough to make out any landmarks. You have no radio, no navigation, no communication. You rely only on your compass to insure that you are traveling in the right direction and that you are holding the precise track that will bring you to your destination. You rely only on your clock to determine how far along your track you have flown and how far you are from your destination.

You know the exact distance you are flying, your exact, true airspeed. Allowing for time to climb, you know exactly how long the flight will take and you note precisely your time of takeoff.

You calculate your compass heading after correcting for magnetic variation and deviation at 47 degrees. So, there you are, watching the clock and the compass, holding your heading precisely at 47 degrees, watching the minutes tick off.

Sooner or later, your attention wanders for too long. You have spent a little too much time watching other instruments to make sure your altitude is right, or simply that you are right side up. Suddenly you notice you are not holding 47 degrees. You are holding 52 degrees, or 57 degrees, or 37 degrees. For how long have you been doing this—five seconds, thirty seconds, five minutes? Do you correct by turning a few degrees in the opposite direction for a few minutes? How long—one minute? Ten? Are you now one-half mile off course, or five miles off course?

Very unsettling in mountainous country, and not much better in the flatlands. If you guess right and correct your course properly, how much extra time has been consumed? While you are figuring out how much additional time is needed before starting the descent to your destination, what do you suppose the chances are that you will continue to hold the precise heading? You no longer know where you are—you're guessing. You come down too early, too late, to the right or to the left of course, with nothing but compass and clock, and you are lost—unless you pinpoint your position by hitting the side of a hill.

Add to this picture the ever-changing, unpredictable winds

and the whole project becomes impossible even for the most precise pilot. The wind is horizontal movement of air and the plane rides on air. When the air mass moves, the plane moves with it. An airplane flies at certain speeds relative to the air. Pilots talk of airspeed and of ground speed. The two are different, and the difference is the wind. If the wind is directly on the nose, or on the tail, it affects only the speed and not the heading a pilot must hold to make good a certain track on the ground.

The wind, however, is rarely right on the nose or the tail. It is seldom so obliging. The greater the angle of wind to our own line of flight, the faster our drift. In clouds, or in reduced visibility, there is no way to notice this drift.

The winds vary not only from one location to the next but also from one altitude to the next. Winds vary in both direction and velocity. There is no way to predict it. There is often very little correlation between the winds forecast by the weather bureau and the actual winds aloft. "Fickle as the wind" is more than just a phrase. The mysteries of the winds have escaped final analysis by the most sophisticated scientific methods available, as have most other aspects of the weather.

For flight in clouds, or above clouds, or without reference to the ground for whatever reason, man is helpless without electronics. He needs his omni—or something like it—to tell him where he is. He needs to know his bearing from a station or, if you prefer, from the various lines leading to a particular ground station he is on. He also needs a bearing from a second station to tell him where he is on that line, or electronic distance-measuring equipment, DME, to tell him the same thing by telling him how many miles he is from the ground station.

As long as the pilot can see the ground, he can sometimes get by with compass and clock—time and distance. When he cannot see the ground, he must have electronic navigation equipment of some type because for instrument flying guessing is not good enough.

Before the student learns to navigate by electronic equipment, he is supposed to learn what it is that the equipment does. He must learn to fly time and distance by compass and clock (in good weather, of course). So he draws a line, figures the true course, the compass variation, the wind drift, and the airspeed. He marks off some checkpoints. He measures the distance between them, and then starts flying—and looking for the checkpoints.

But not always do they come up when they're supposed to. The best points to use are those directly along the line of flight, rather than points to the right or left. It is much easier to check distance and, consequently, your ground speed, when the checkpoint is directly along your flight path. Such points, of course, should come up right on the nose. More likely, you will find them to your right or left; sometimes, not at all.

A bridge, the intersection of two highways, or a TV station is sometimes hard to spot. So you just keep going and hope that you can spot the final checkpoint, your airport of destination, somewhere within your range of vision. You hope that the wind has not blown you too far or that you have not been too careless. With no radio navigation equipment, you need some good luck.

Looking for checkpoints is similar to another form of initiation into the art of aerial navigation known as pilotage.

Pilotage is the most primitive form of navigation. It is also the simplest. Pilotage is the kind of navigation the pilot uses when he follows the Interstate from one city to the next, or follows the railroad tracks, or a river, or powerlines. He will follow the Interstate to a certain town, which can be identified by two large lakes just north of the town, to take one example, then the westbound set of railroad tracks out of town until it joins a dirt road. Then he follows the dirt road to the airport he is looking for. If there is no continuous road, railroad, river, or power line, he picks out points about ten miles apart.

Pilotage is easy. By the time you get to one landmark you can see the next. Sometimes, if your checkpoints are close enough together, you can see the next two. No matter how you handle it, pilotage is very simple.

But somehow I've never been able to do it. I have to have an omni, or at least a low-frequency automatic direction finder. Otherwise I am practically certain to get lost. Pilotage is not my cup of tea. The ground just doesn't look like the map and the map just doesn't look like the ground. The problem, at least in part, is that there never has been, and never will be, a map that has anywhere near as much detail as the ground.

I've looked for a set of railroad tracks running out of a particular town to the east and I've seen three sets of tracks. Instead of the one highway prominently shown on the map, I've seen six. Sometimes the map shows three highways and by studying it, I can see that the one I want parallels the railroad track for about the first ten miles out of town. So all I have to do is look for the road with the railroad tracks beside it and follow that one.

So I do. I spot the road with the railroad tracks along its side. But after five miles or so, after the other roads have veered off and are lost in the brush, or the haze, I see that the railroad track is not a railroad track—it's a ditch, or a levee. From 3,000 feet or more, how do you tell? I've mistaken telephone lines for railroads and canals for rivers.

In obedience to my map, I have picked out *the* road with a river following alongside. There could be no doubt that the river was parallel to my road just like the map showed; except the river I picked was *not* shown on the map—it was too narrow and insignificant. Everybody knows you can't show every little stream on the map because there wouldn't be room for anything else. The map showed a much bigger stream that paralleled another road out of town—the road I wanted. But seeing a stream beside a road, I followed that road—the one I didn't want—and I got lost.

In later years, I once followed a mountain valley in Colorado and had intentions of turning north along another valley when I reached a certain town. Because of the high mountains, the omni is of little use in parts of Colorado. It was going to be really easy to pick this town out because the town was a yellow splotch on the map. That meant it was a town of over 25,000 people. All the other towns I would fly over along this valley were simply circles, or circles with dots. Anyone can tell a yellow splotch from a circle. What I didn't realize was that the yellow splotch might have 25,150 people and the circle with a dot might have 24,850 people. At 2,000 feet above the valley floor, you can't see any people, and you wouldn't have time to count them if you could. I got lost again.

Trying to pick out an ordinary road in most parts of the country is like playing grab bag. There are roads everywhere. The maps used for this kind of flying come out only once every year and a half, and the highway departments don't stop building roads when the new maps come out.

Following the Interstate north for a hundred miles or so to an airport sounds like a snap. To some pilots it is, but not to me. The town may be six cities up, and I tend to lose count. Besides, one of them looks so small, it probably wasn't on the map—or was it? Did I pass four or five towns? According to the map, the airport is about three miles east of the city. There's an airport off to the east of this one, but there is a little lake right next to it that my map doesn't show. Is it the wrong town, and airport, or was the little lake too little to put on the map?

You can have it. I like to look at the ground when I fly, but only because it looks so appealing, not to figure out where I am. I don't like to follow highways or railroads and I don't like to look for roadside diners. From the air they look just like laundries.

I like to fly by the numbers. If you are careful, the 250-degree radial on your omni bearing selector doesn't look like any other radial. You can always distinguish one number from the other. Twenty miles on the distance-measuring equipment can't be mistaken for any other distance. There is only one needle on the omni and I can't mistake it for any other.

I suppose I ought to think about all of that when I think about the good old days in the late fifties when I flew planes without radios. I suppose I should remember all the gnawing doubts that accompanied the exhilaration of solitude. The knowledge that I was truly out of contact with every living soul and unreachable until I was close enough to the airport to see a light signal from the man in the tower was a good part of the joy of flight. But maybe it was not as good as it seems.

The day came when the word went out that all planes based at the field would have to be equipped with two-way radios. They weren't requiring navigation equipment. The government didn't care if we got lost, they just didn't want us to collide with anybody while taking off or landing, and they wanted us in continual radio contact with the tower when within five miles of the airport if we were flying below 2,000 feet.

But the navcoms were sold as a unit. Either you couldn't buy the com without the nav, or it was economically unsound to do so. Whatever the reason, the owner of the flight school equipped all his planes with navcoms. He fussed and fumed and swore that the government was trying to drive the little operators out of business. He said it was impractical. He said it was unnecessary. But he bought the navcoms.

The little black boxes came to my rescue. With a little instruction and a little practice, I soon learned that I could fly from one place to another without looking at the ground. It was thrilling. I did look at the ground, of course, and not only because it is so enticing from several thousand feet up but also because I got a perverse pleasure out of looking and realizing that the omni—the all-knowing, never-failing, omniscient, omnipotent omni—was taking me to my destination over a route that didn't look right. I always seemed to be going the wrong way, at least by 20 or 40 degrees, and I knew that without that little gadget I would have done a lot of extra flying and endured a lot of uncertainty before finding my destination. I trusted the black box implicitly. I was enthralled by its magic. I loved being led along courses that look wrong, while knowing I must be going right.

Of course, I could have put my time to better use. I should have studied my chart to see why we went the route we did. Certainly, I should have tried to determine my precise position at all times and to correlate landmarks on the ground with marks on the map. It would all have been good insurance against the day when the omni, like all electronic gadgets, might suddenly get tired and quit. Mercifully, in those early days of my career it never did.

Unfortunately, I never got a chance to get really used to it. A combined shortage of time and money made me decide to take a temporary breather from flying. I had a private license and about 130 hours logged. I was working toward a commercial license when I decided to give it up for a while. I told everyone, myself included, that it was temporary. Just a breather. I planned to start again soon. I said it so often that people quit asking me when I was going back to flying, but I really intended to go back.

One day, I took my son, then eight years old, to a kite-flying party. In short order, the kite wound up in a tree. My son's chagrin at the loss of the kite was matched only by his disappointment at the ineptitude of his father. "Never mind kites," I assured him. I had something much better in mind. How would he like to do some real flying? How would he like to be up there looking down instead of down here looking up? He looked as excited as I felt at the prospect.

We went to the Lakefront Airport. The old flying school was out of business. I wondered silently if it was the cost of the radios that did it, but we soon found another operator willing to rent us a plane and pilot. I was licensed myself, I informed the pilot. Perhaps, after we were safely aloft and level, I might handle the controls. My captain was obliging. How long had it been since I had flown? A number of years now, I replied.

It felt good to handle the controls again, but the rust was evident. I made arrangements to come back for refamiliarization, as they call it, and to continue with a commercial course.

When I got home, I looked up the old log books and checked the last entry. It had been nine years.

IV

Needles and Dials

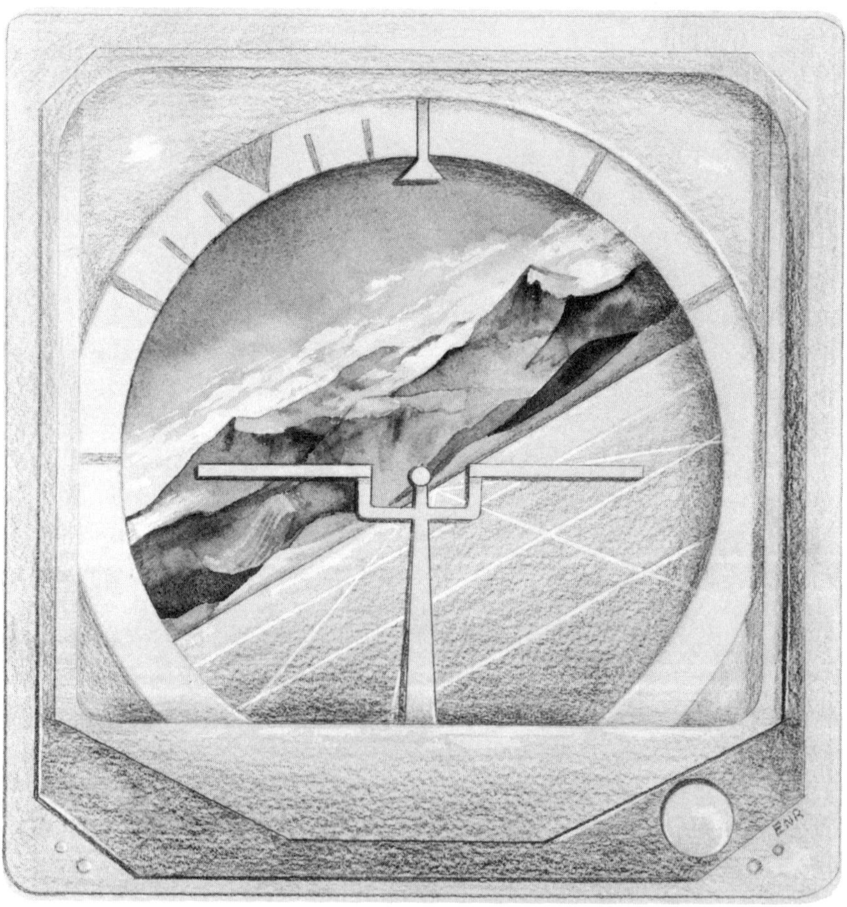
ENR

The dangers that we know about when embarking on a new adventure are only a part of our fears. The biggest part of our trepidation is the dangers that we cannot anticipate. The fact that we do not have the solution to known dangers has always held less terror than has the possible existence of a danger whose nature could not be known, or even guessed.

When men first left the ground in heavier-than-air machines, many of the problems and risks were obvious enough. What was neither obvious nor anticipated was the solid barriers to flight imposed by the airy, fluffy, often harmless-looking visible moisture known as clouds. The first men to fly could never have known that the inside of the most benign-looking clouds held insidious dangers, and that the world of flight they looked forward to exploring was, in fact, two worlds. Only through mastery of that second world—the world of clouds—can come the almost limitless freedom that the early pilots set out to find.

The early pilots did not know, but student pilots today do. They know because it is ingrained in them from the first day. "Stay clear of clouds," they are told. "Take care not to stumble into them." As students we were told of two dangers. The first was collision with another aircraft. This was possible, but most unlikely. The other was loss of control, for reasons that we did not, as new students, fully understand. This consequence was stated to be almost a certainty.

The new pilot is taught to stay out of the clouds the way a young child is taught to stay out of the street. New pilots are limited to flying by visual flight rules. VFR is his sidewalk. Conditions requiring instrument flight rules (IFR) are forbidden territory. VFR and IFR thus become part of his vocabulary. To enter that second world without preparation and skill is dangerous. To enter it without a certificate from the government and a clearance from the FAA is illegal.

When the ceiling, the base of clouds covering at least 60 percent of the sky, is below 1,000 feet above the surface at the airport, or when visibility is less than three miles, the sky is closed to the VFR pilot. Under these conditions there is only one world of flight—that second world that only the duly certified may enter. When the ceiling lifts, or visibility improves, the VFR pilot may venture forth, but under certain rather stringent guidelines. He may not enter clouds, nor may he fly prohibitively close to them. He must stay 500 feet below, 1,000 feet on top, or 2,000 feet horizontally from them.

The sky is full of traps for the VFR pilot. To dodge the white puffs is relatively easy, if sometimes annoying, but lowering ceilings can force the pilot to continually lower altitude, a bad enough situation over the flatlands and worse still over rising terrain. Lowering ceilings or gradually reducing visibility can creep up on the unwary pilot until he becomes aware quite suddenly and without prior apprehension that he has unwittingly stumbled into that other, forbidden place. Or the blanket may form silently beneath him, covering with white the destination that was clear at the time of takeoff.

As a new pilot I did as I was told. My instructors had made their point well. I learned, as did most new students, to fear the most cursory brush with clouds. We were told to run at the first sign of potential unavoidable contact.

The first sign came early. On a cross-country flight in an 85 hp Luscombe without radio, I got an unexpected view of a cloud blanket from above and went into headlong retreat back to the safety of the Lakefront Airport. I had intended to fly to Hammond, about fifteen miles northwest of Lake Pontchartrain. Our airport is on the southeast shore of the lake. I was going to follow the south shore, turning north along a narrow strip of land that divides Lake Pontchartrain from Lake Maurepaus, to the west.

But as I approached that narrow strip of land, I could not see it. I saw only solid white beneath. I did not know and did not wait to find out what lay ahead. The loss of sight of the familiar earth even temporarily was enough. I turned around and was relieved to see the home field still in bright sunshine and to see that I was not trapped above the clouds.

But a few months later, on a return flight from Mobile, Alabama, I did indeed find myself trapped above an almost solid layer that was not supposed to be there. With no omni, I was flying by compass and clock, dead reckoning, but a break in the overcast revealed only water where I had not reckoned it to be.

Obviously I had drifted south—how far, I had no way of knowing. I selected the biggest hole I could find, even though it lay farther south, farther out over the water. I spiraled through it, taking care not to touch the poisonous substance around me, no matter how steep a bank it required. I had visions of being out of range of land, halfway to Mexico, maybe. That is the problem with being lost above clouds. You sometimes muse over the possibility that you will emerge underneath to find yourself on another planet. I knew I really could not be far from land, but it was an undeniable relief to see it a few miles to the north as I leveled below the clouds.

Upon returning to flying after my long layoff, another planned trip was aborted when I was unable to avoid the growing balls of cotton east of the city. I carefully treaded my way around them, but when, despite my care, one hit me in the face, I decided it was time to go back.

I also decided that if I were going to continue flying, I would have to get an instrument rating. You are simply too restricted without it. If you are going to do any serious traveling with an airplane, familiarity and mastery of that other world of flight becomes a necessity.

Is it really so different?

It is different indeed. That first world offers simply a new perspective of the one we know from birth: the earth, the sky, and the line where they meet called the horizon. It is looking down on a familiar earth from which we formerly looked up at a familiar sky. It is an expanded horizon—but still a horizon. It is a different view of the world, but still a world clearly recognizable.

But the world of IFR is different. It is a strange universe for which the uninitiated have no frame of reference. There is no earth, no sky, and no horizon. It is a world of numbers and symbols, needles and dials, frequencies and dots and dashes, a voice on the radio and nothing else.

There is no fast or slow; there is a needle that moves to a higher or lower number on a dial. There is no up or down; there is another needle that silently oscillates up or down from the horizontal. There are no level or banked conditions; there is a straight line that rolls, in a circular face, from a horizontal position toward the vertical. A pointer at the top of the circular face moves along a series of hash marks telling you more or less precisely how much toward the vertical the line has moved.

How do you turn right or left? You don't. You don't move at all. Only the needles move. You apply certain pressures to certain controls and the needle moves right or left.

North or south? East or west? This way or that way? There is no this way or that. There are numbers on a compass. Are you high or low? No, you are not; you are neither. There is no high or low, only numbers. The numbers may be too high or too low, but not you. You are in the center of your world—in fact, you are the only thing in it. The plane is just an extension of your hands and feet and the instruments extensions of your nerves.

This is insane. You must know if you are going straight or turning without looking at an instrument. You must know if you are going up or down, or if you are straight or on your side. These are simply natural sensations that every human being learns from infancy.

The sensations are indeed natural, but the world of instrument flight is not. When you enter the milky white world of IFR you leave your natural sensations behind. These trusted instincts and natural reactions that have served you so well as a ground animal, and in the familiar world of VFR, will betray you and lead you to grief in the world of IFR. When the sensations that you have blindly obeyed since you were old enough to remember reassure you that you are straight and level and that all is right, do not believe them. Ignore them. Ignore the sensations you have always obeyed without question, without hesitation, and without conscious thought.

When instinct screams that you are going too fast and that you are diving straight down toward disaster, turn a deaf ear. Forget everything you have learned about up and down, straight and turning, level and leaning—everything that has seeped deep into your unconscious, become part of your fiber, and kept you alive and well.

Believe your instruments. Believe your mechanical, electrical, gyroscopic, magnetic, and mass-produced instruments. Ignore your intelligence and believe the dial on the panel in front of you.

Are you moving in a straight line—exactly in the direction in which you were going when you entered the clouds a few minutes ago? Good! Do your wings feel like they are parallel to the earth? Does your nose point straight ahead without seeming to move right or left? Good! You do not even seem to be going up or down. Everything is in place and all's right in the world.

So what do you do about the fact that the turn needle has crept over to the right, that the line on the artificial horizon dips slightly toward the left? What does it mean that the numbers on the compass are slowly increasing, that the numbers on the airspeed indicator slowly increase as the numbers on the altimeter become slowly smaller?

Do you ignore it? Not if you want to keep flying. Not if you want to keep living. We're not talking now merely about finding your way to Peoria without getting lost. We're talking about staying right side up as opposed to upside down, about keeping the plane in one piece as opposed to pulling it apart.

Do you find that hard to understand? So did those intrepid adventurers in the early days of flight. Blithely, without fear or hesitation, they flew their fragile craft into the clouds. Those who survived by bailing out all told the same story: the plane flew fine until they entered the overcast, then everything went to pot—the plane went crazy, the controls didn't work anymore.

As soon as they flew into the soup, nothing seemed to be the same. The speed would increase and they lost altitude. They knew that much because an airspeed indicator and an altimeter were two of the few instruments the early pilots had. Besides, they could tell it by the increased pitch of the sound of the prop and the sound of the wires humming in the wind. So they did what they always did: they eased back a little on the yoke. More back pressure on the yoke, which moves the elevators and keeps the nose up, increases the angle of attack, increases lift, and stops a descent; but more back pressure on the yoke also increases drag and causes the speed to drop. This procedure was fine as long as they could see what they were dong. But somehow in clouds it doesn't work. Back pressure might slow the speed momentarily, but then it picked up even more. And the early pilots started losing altitude faster. Obviously they were in a dive, so they pulled back harder.

But the more they pulled back the faster the crazy thing went. The speed and the sound went beyond anything the pilot had experienced in clear skies. In desperation, sometimes in panic, the hapless pilot yanked back on the controls. The wings usually went first. Sometimes parts of the tail section. According to eyewitness accounts, only pieces came out of the clouds, followed by a parachute. Sometimes, no parachute.

These early fliers, undoubtedly to a man, pulled their planes to pieces thinking they were diving wings-level toward the ground. They were not. Aeronautical investigation and experimentation soon proved that these unknowing adventurers had pulled their planes to pieces in tight, steeply banked descending turns known as spirals, "graveyard spirals," as they aptly became known.

It still happens today with surprising frequency. Accident reports still tell of planes undergoing "structural failure" because the pilot continued into "adverse weather conditions beyond his experience/capability level." It is surprising because even the early pilots soon learned to stay out of an overcast. When the ceiling lowered, making visual contact impossible, they would console each other with the news that "even the birds are walking." This apparently lessened the humiliation of being grounded. From the literature, it seems that pilots have long soothed their bruised egos with the observation "even the birds are walking."

But why do pilots go into spirals when they cannot see the ground? And, why do they not know it when they do? In answering these two questions, aviation researchers learned much about planes and men.

Some of the very qualities that make the flying machine manageable in "normal" visual flight helped to make it a trap when the first pilots ventured into clouds.

If you take your hands and feet off the controls of an airplane, no matter how aerodynamically stable and expertly trimmed, it will fly straight only until the first trace of turbulence or rough air. To fly perfectly straight, even the perfectly trimmed plane needs perfectly still air, and this rarely exists except for very short periods of time over very small areas. If there's the slightest roughness in the air, caused by unevenness of the terrain or building clouds, one wing will drop. When one wing drops for more than just a very few degrees, the plane will turn. The bank of the wing is what makes an airplane turn.

Straight and level flight has been defined as an infinite number of small corrections in heading and altitude. It is a never-ending series of minute climbs, descents, and turns to heading. It is no different from driving a car. Theoretically, the wheels are supposed to be aligned and if you take your hands off the wheel, the car go straight, as long as the road does.

But it is a far from perfect world, on the highways as well as in the skies, and driving straight, like flying straight, is a continual series of minor corrections. We are continually nudging the plane or the car into line, but we have to see the line—the highway, or the stripe down the middle of it if we are driving, or the imaginary line to the next landmark if we are flying. Without an outside reference, there is no such thing as straight. Men lost in the desert have been known to walk in giant circles thinking they were walking straight.

Imagine yourself driving along a highway, a perfectly straight highway with no guardrail and nothing but deep water on either side of the road. If you are a driver of even minimal skill, it presents no problem. You just drive straight along the highway and you will stay out of the water.

Now suppose you come to a long stretch where the water, for

some reason, covers the road, either because the road is lower, or the water is higher. Imagine it is dirty water that you can't see through, so you cannot see the road—either ahead or beneath you. For as far as you can see, the road is covered with water—only a few inches of it, but to all appearances, you are in the middle of a lake of uniform depth. All you see is a surface of what appears to be one large body of water.

It should not be too bad. You know the deep water is off to either side of you, but you know that the highway continues straight ahead and that it is covered by only a few inches of it. So all you have to do is to drive straight and you are safe. Just do not let the car turn, that's all.

Just make it go straight. How do you do that without a reference? Do you grip the wheel tightly to prevent the car from turning the slightest fraction of a degree? Do you hold it loosely so as to sense and then correct any movement?

It does not matter. Anyone who has any experience driving a car and who thinks about this mythical predicament at all will know that the only thing to do is to stop and turn off the switch. It is better to walk and feel your way one step at a time. Try driving and you will be off the side of the road, under deep water, within a matter of minutes, if not seconds.

But our mythical driver has it easy compared to the early pilots who flew into the clouds. He has it easier on two counts. First, the driver is in a two-dimensional world. He does not have to worry about up and down. Second, the steering mechanism of a car is designed so that the car "wants" to go straight. It takes force to turn the wheel; and when you let it go, the steering wheel and, consequently, the front wheels of the car, tend to straighten out.

Airplanes aren't built that way. They are built for stability in all phases of flight, including turns. They *do* have a built-in stability for straight and level flight, and following a *slight* jar from turbulence or gustiness of the air, the plane will, through built-in aerodynamic stability, tend to return to level flight.

But once the plane is banked more than just a few degrees, it will not tend to return to normal flight at all. It will stay banked and continue the turn that always results from a bank. With the controls neutral, the plane will continue to turn. Unless the pilot rolls the plane out of the bank, and consequently out of the turn, the plane will stay banked and keep turning.

The inherent stability for level flight is overcome by the increased lift on the high wing. The high wing is the one on the outside of the turn and it gets more lift because it is moving faster than the inside. In fact, as the turn gets steeper, there is an overbanking tendency resulting from this higher speed and greater lift on the high wing. The pilot has to hold his controls against the turn as though turning in the opposite direction just to keep the same degree of bank. If he does not, the bank will continue to steepen until the wings approach the vertical.

When the plane turns, things happen. G forces increase and the plane starts to lost altitude. The nose immediately drops in response. As we have seen, it drops because the plane is built to maintain the same relative angle between the wind and the wing. The plane has a built-in stability for this "angle of attack," so the nose drops and the speed builds.

As speed increases, the pilot will instinctively pull back on the controls to lower the speed by keeping the nose up. Up? As far as the plane's elevators are concerned, up is toward the ceiling of the cabin, or the top of the head of a pilot in an open cockpit. The airplane's controls do not know where the earth is. They only know the top and bottom of the plane. During a turn, "up" means, partially, farther away from the ground; but it also means, in part, farther toward the inside of the turn. "Up" elevator in a turn tightens the turn.

When the pilot can see, he instinctively corrects for that by holding enough opposite aileron to prevent any tightening of the turn. He doesn't want to tighten his turn, he just wants to keep his nose from dropping toward the earth. He wants to hold his altitude. So he will keep the same amount of bank by proper use of his aileron control—that is, he will keep the horizon at the same angle in his windshield, while he keeps the nose on the horizon, or the same distance above it, with the elevator control.

That is what he will do when he can see the horizon, or at

least the earth, or a glimpse of it. When he cannot see, he must fly instruments. The early pilots had no instruments to tell them whether they were turning, but they did not think them necessary. They relied on their ability to fly by the seat of their pants. Unfortunately, there is no way to fly instruments *by* the seat of your pants.

"Seat-of-the-pants" flying is really a very accurate and descriptive term. If you flew with your right wing low, you would slide toward the right of your seat and you would feel friction in the seat of your pants. If you entered a turn only by banking the wing and without using the rudders to assist, you would momentarily tend to slip to the inside of the turn and you would feel it in the seat of your pants—just as you do in a car when you go very slowly around a steeply banked roadway turn. If you used too much rudder for the amount of the bank, you would skid toward the outside of the turn and you would feel it in the seat of your pants—just as you do in a car if you make a fast turn in a roadway that is banked too little or not at all.

As long as these early pioneers were seated firmly in their seats, they figured everything must be okay. But whenever they flew into clouds, it wasn't. It was the same old story. Unbeknown to the pilots, the plane started a very gentle turn, the nose dropped, and speed increased; the pilot pulled back to keep the nose "up." He knew the nose was dropping, but he didn't know the plane was turning. He had no way of knowing that. If a plane starts to turn because of a gust or other natural cause and not by use of the ailerons, there is not even the momentary slip and no need for rudders to stop it. So everything was fine except that the speed kept increasing. And the pilot kept pulling the nose "up." And the turn, the perfectly coordinated turn, which the pilot didn't even know he was in, kept tightening as the nose dropped farther and the speed increased. If the pilot pulled back farther on his elevator controls, still trying to keep the nose "up," the turn tightened more.

G forces built up—beyond the structural strength of the plane. Or the speed built up until it went beyond the plane's capacity, and the whole thing came apart.

But the pilot! Why didn't the pilot know he was turning? Why did the seat of his pants not tell him? How is it that a man could not tell in some way that he is turning, rather than moving in a straight line? What happens to his sense of balance—that delicate mechanism of fluid in the inner ear?

According to the doctors, it is this fluid in the inner ear that tells you when you are leaning. It is what keeps you right side up. When something goes wrong with this mechanism, you are subject to that affliction known as vertigo—you get dizzy and lose your balance. Sometimes you cannot tell if you are upright or leaning and you fall. Because of this sense of balance, the passenger in an automobile knows he is leaning and off balance, even if he does not feel it in the seat of his pants, or cannot see it.

But in a turning airplane it is different. The pilot is not thrown to the outside of the turn, because the plane banks as it turns. The bank is what makes it turn.

The pilot will be thrown neither right nor left. He will be pressed back into his seat just like a passenger in a car accelerating in a straight line. Since "acceleration" is defined by the physicist as a change in speed or direction, in a car, or a plane, if the bank is right, a turn feels just like an increase in speed. If the bank is exactly proportionate to the turn, the passenger is thrown neither to the outside nor the inside of the turn, and unless he can see, he senses the acceleration only as a change in speed.

Even when the early aircraft designers pinpointed the problem, it was not easy to find a solution. The plane turned by banking; centrifugal force was counterbalanced and both the pilot and every mechanical gadget he tried to devise remained perfectly upright relative to the airplane. Some pilots tried tying a piece of string to the wing strut hoping to see the string skid one way or the other to indicate a turn, but the string stayed with the plane, always stretched straight back from the strut. It showed only the angle of the wind to the wing, a perpendicular movement. Whether the plane was flying straight or turning made no difference to the string. Neither the string nor any other device would "lean" to give the pilot an indication that he was turning. Even the water in a glass would stay level. They all remained in the same relative position, all equally balanced by the bank and turn. All but one.

The one gadget that was finally discovered that did not behave like the others was a gyro, which is like a top that kids use as a toy. A rapidly spinning object for some reason has a mind of its own. It will stay upright regardless of the platform on which it is mounted—rigidity in space, the physicists call it. Spin a top on a flat board; then, while the top is spinning, tilt the board. The top does not tilt with it. It stays perpendicular to the ground. Only when it stops spinning does the top tumble.

The pilots now had a reference to the outside world. The rest was simple. The men who first utilized the spinning gyros in aircraft became the big names in the growing industry of aircraft instruments.

Mount a gyro to an instrument in the panel. Create a vacuum to keep the gyros spinning. Operate the vacuum pump electrically or with the force of moving air from outside the fuselage by means of a venturi tube. Or use an engine-driven suction pump. By means of a system of levers attached from the gyro mechanism to an instrument on the face of the panel, the pilot could, at last, tell the attitude of his plane with reference to the horizon, whether he could see the horizon or not. Whether the plane was in clear skies or solid clouds didn't make the slightest bit of difference to the spinning gyro. To the pilot in the clouds, the gyro was a lifeline to the real world.

If the plane turned, a needle on a dial moved from the upright to one side to tell the pilot he was turning and in which direction. Using gyros, the engineers also developed for the pilot an "artificial horizon." If the plane banked, the pilot knew it because the line on the panel representing the horizon tilted to one side. It did not really tilt. The line stayed steady, parallel to the real horizon. It was the airplane that tilted around the ever-steady artificial horizon, but to the pilot, who turned with the plane, it appeared to be the line that was tilting.

The same instrument told the pilot when his nose was moving

up and when it was moving down. If the plane's nose moved up 10 degrees from the horizon, the line stayed where it was, and to the pilot, it appeared that the line had moved down on the face of his instrument.

The engineers also fashioned a gyro compass. The magnetic compass always points north and theoretically will always tell the pilot which way his nose is pointed. Unfortunately, that is true only when the plane is flying straight and level and in still air. If the air is turbulent, the compass card will bounce back and forth in the fluid in which it is suspended. Pilots learned to take an "average reading," but this was a rough approximation of an airplane's heading at best.

An even bigger problem was the turn. When the plane banks, the compass swings, and during a turn, depending on the heading and direction of the turn, races ahead of the nose, or lags markedly behind it. So it gives no clear indication of how fast the plane is turning even in still air. Worse, sometimes at the start of a turn from a northerly heading, the compass will momentarily show a turn in the opposite direction. It is not a very reliable indication of how much of a turn is being made or when the pilot should stop his turn to roll out on the desired heading.

But the gyro compass, set to the proper heading against the magnetic compass when the wings are level and the air is still, will stay upright at least for a reasonable length of time after being set. It will accurately show heading at all times throughout the turn, no matter how steep, and no matter how much the plane is bounced around by turbulence.

This was a truly remarkable breakthrough. By looking at his turn indicator and his artificial horizon, the pilot could know exactly his attitude with reference to the ground, though he could see nothing beyond the tips of his wings. That other world, beyond the visual, was now open to conquest. The gyro had eliminated its terrors. But the transition to instruments was not quite as easy as one might expect. Old habits die hard.

Man had been used to living by his senses and he did not take quickly or easily to following the commands of needles and dials, especially when they contradicted what he felt. If he felt he was right side up, it was not easy to move the controls to the left because a needle or a little white line said you were banked and turning to the right. If he did move the controls to the left, then it felt as if he were trying to turn left, and when the needle straightened out, he felt as if he were in a continuing left turn. New pilots being taught "blind flying," as they called it, would, in such circumstances unconsciously lean to the right. By the exercise of sheer will, they would keep the needle centered, showing level flight, though every instinct inside them said they were turning left.

For the old seat-of-the-pants pilots, it was even harder. They would complain that these new gyro instruments only worked in clear skies, that as soon as you went into a cloud, the crazy gadget showed a turn, although you were "obviously" going straight.

The illusions and false sensations of instrument flight are endless. They haunt the new pilot in a thousand ways. Every pilot who wants to get serious about flying must learn to fly twice, once in the visual world and then in the world of instruments. I learned this as an instrument student and I learned it again as an instrument instructor.

More and more the emphasis is on introducing the new student to instruments from the very start. Even new students are put under the "hood" for an hour or two and some hood time is now required even for a private license. The "hood" is a piece of plastic or similar material worn like a cap. It has a visor designed to be long enough and wide enough to cut off all vision outside the plane's cabin, but to permit a full view of the instrument panel. An instructor or safety pilot sits in the right seat.

Students and licensed instrument pilots make frequent use of the hood. For proficiency on instruments, continued practice is necessary (six hours in six months is the minimum FAA requirement), but clouds don't always appear when you want them to, or for as long as you'd like. When they are solid and lasting they may contain embedded thunderstorms, which are never wanted, and even when they do not hide storms, you cannot roam about in clouds at will. You cannot enter clouds without an FAA clearance, and a clearance involves straight and level flight from one place to another. A clearance does not permit practice turns of varying steepness, straight flight at varying speeds or climbs and descents—all maneuvers that must be mastered by the student under the hood.

So the pilot's lingo has come to include not only IFR but two other terms that more frequently take its place. Instead of IFR, pilots usually speak of "hood time" and "actual time." Except for pros, who fly many hours a month, most pilots will have more hood time than actual instrument time. Often no more than 10 to 15 percent of a pilot's flight time will be actual IFR. There just aren't enough clouds. During fall and winter in the Midwest and the Northeast there may be much opportunity for actual IFR, but for months on end in the Southwest pilots may have no opportunity to stay current without using the hood.

Instrument flight is no longer the mystery it once was, nor does it inspire the awe in the new pilot that "blind flying" did in previous decades. Professional flying today in unthinkable without instruments, though in some limited forms, still technically legal. But it is instrument flight that has made the business of air transport possible.

Instrument flying is still the *ne plus ultra* of the airman's art. Among amateurs, it still separates those who fly cross-country as a hobby from those who do it as a serious avocation. Except for specialized skills such as aerobatics or crop dusting, instrument flying is still the most difficult and the most demanding skill that the pilot acquires. Even a pilot who is reasonably proficient in visual flight has not, through that skill alone, sufficiently overcome the deep-seated obedience to his instincts; nor sufficiently used to living or ordering his life according to needles and dials.

Consider, for example, the tendency of all propeller planes to yaw and roll to the left during a climb. It takes much pressure on the right rudder to keep the plane straight. As long as the fledgling pilot can see that the pressure he exerts with his right leg is keeping the plane climbing straight, he will exert that pressure no matter how sore it makes his leg. Put a hood on him and cut out his vision from the outside world and he does not want to press so hard on that right rudder for it feels, for all the world, as if he is turning hard right when he does so. The needles say that he is going straight, but he feels as if he is turning right. And more than once, after I started giving instructions to students under the hood, I noticed a student leaning unconsciously to his left as he pressed on the right rudder, needlessly compensating for an imagined turn to the right.

Even that is progress, however. At first the student will repeatedly allow the plane to slide. He will avoid the uncomfortable pressure on the right leg and allow the plane to skid, happy in his instinctive feeling that he is climbing straight.

The pilot must learn not only to disregard his instincts but to obey the instructions of his instruments, and the peculiar language and limitations of each. He must correlate one with the other. And he must learn to scan, and not to become absorbed in any of them to the exclusion of the others.

To become absorbed with a single instrument is easy to do. Your outside reference has been cut out. You are in a noisy, vibrating machine that exists in a three-dimensional medium. In place of the missing horizon that tells you almost everything you need to know are numerous needles and dials, most of which convey only one isolated scrap of information each. None of them alone conveys very much.

So when you see that you are starting to climb and that you are already slightly high, you become absorbed in correcting your altitude and in holding it. And sometimes you become so absorbed you do not see that you have turned 40 degrees or 90 degrees off course, until your instructor or safety pilot intervenes. A complete, unconscious 360-degree turn by a new instrument student is not unknown.

I once saw a student so absorbed with holding his heading that altimeter, air speed, rate of climb indicator, and artificial horizon were all but forgotten till the stall-warning horn sounded as the speed bled dangerously away, as the nose pointed high in the sky, and the altimeter showed that we had climbed over 500 feet. Any one of these instruments would have showed him that he had departed from level flight, which he was supposed to be practicing.

After level flight is mastered come turns, descents, climbs, climbing turns, descending turns, changes of airspeed in level flight, and changes of airspeed while turning. Each requires primary reference to a different instrument as well as secondary or backup information from other instruments. There is a correct order of instrument scan for each regimen of flight. When these simple elements of flight are mastered, the pilot must then practice and learn the one maneuver it is all intended to accomplish—the flight from here to there.

Follow another needle—the omni—another needle at which to stare, to the total disregard of everything else. By the time you start a student on the omni under the hood you think the obedience to the needles of the attitude instruments has become second nature. Sometimes you find it has not. But sooner or later it must. It must become instinctive to keep the plane steady while tracking the omni or obeying the command of the ground controller: Turn right headed 330 degrees, climb to and maintain 5,000 feet. Descend to 4,000 feet; turn left heading 020 degrees; reduce speed to 120 knots; turn left heading 140 degrees; join the localizer course.

This localizer course is a course on which two electronic beams converge along an extension of the center line of an instrument-equipped runway. It is also a tightrope. Instrument flying is like walking a plank. It is learning not to correct an incipient fall to one side of the plank by leaning too far to the other; not to overcorrect; not to fall off the left side trying to avoid the right. Small movements; small corrections.

When the student is placed on the localizer course for the first time, the plank is taken away, and in its place is the tightrope. This string, the localizer, is part of an instrument landing system (ILS), which allows the pilot to approach the runway from many miles out and to line up precisely with it, through clouds, fog, haze, or any other obstruction to visibility. Its signals are read from the same omni instrument that the pilot uses to guide his craft from one station to the other, except that the only course on the localizer frequency is the center line of the runway, and the localizer signal is four times as sensitive as the omni. The tightrope, in other words, is one-fourth as wide as the plank the student is used to.

While flying an omni course, as the needle reaches full deflection to one side of the instrument, the pilot is 10 degrees off course, the full swing of the needle from one side to the other representing 20 degrees. A full deflection of the localizer's needle comes when it's only 2½ degrees off course, the full swing of the needle representing only 5 degrees. If the pilot uses the same amount of correction to center the omni, he will soon see his needle swinging wildly to the other side of his instrument as he shoots through the beam and falls off his tightrope. It takes practice.

But the ILS is two tightropes. The second is one that finds no metaphor among earth-bound people. It is the vertical string, the one that gives the pilot vertical guidance to the surface at the runway's threshold. It is just as difficult to follow. This "glide scope" needle moves vertically across the face of the same instrument and the pilot must center not one needle, but two—one horizontally, one vertically.

It is better to learn one at a time. Most instructors will have their students first fly the localizer course at a constant, high altitude, not worrying about descent. Only after students have achieved reasonable proficiency in staying on the localizer course will they be permitted to start a descent to the runway and practice with the second, the vertical needle.

The start of this descent is signaled in the plane by a flashing blue light on the panel and a series of beeps from the audio portion of the marker beacon instrument in the plane. Both signals are activated by a ground transmitter, known as the outer marker, located usually four or five miles from the runway threshold, as the plane passes overhead. The glide scope needle is kept centered by maintaining a steady rate of descent, just as the localizer needle is centered by a constant track over the ground.

Once more the student is confronted with needles that demand his attention. Needles that threaten to disconcert him from everything else with the slightest lapse of diligence. As a student I once became so absorbed in following this localizer on the approach under the hood, that I ignored the marker, the flashing light, the beeping sound, the falling glide scope needle, and flew right over the airport at 2,000 feet, delighted with the centered localizer needle. As an instructor, I admit to a perverse satisfaction in seeing one of my students once do the same thing.

I have seen still others do S-turns with ever expanding loops as they sporadically note the swing of the localizer needle, for their attention has been riveted on the glide scope. On other occasions they will roller-coaster down the glide path, first above, then below, with their primary focus on the localizer. Like everything else in this three-dimensional domain, sooner or later it comes together.

ILS is the most accurate system, but not the only type of instrument approach. There are others utilizing the omni for guidance to the runway, or a nondirectional beacon (NDB) permitting use by the pilot of his automatic direction finder, a needle that points to the NDB, wherever the plane may be, and the most difficult and least accurate of the approaches.

The instrument pilot has to learn them all. The instrument approach is the most difficult aspect of instrument flying. It requires precision. It means, as a rule, a number of turns, changes in altitude and, finally, a continuous rate of descent and exact directional control to the runway. During most phases of flight, not all of the instruments are conveying information that must be immediately monitored. Often, some needles may be ignored. But on the approach the whole orchestra is playing; every instrument shouts at you. Practically every instrument, every needle, and every dial spews out data vitally affecting the correct interpretation of the others.

Somewhere along that final descent path, along the approach to the runway, the plane will fly out of the nether world of gauges and reenter the familiar environment of ground and sky. The pilot will observe movement and see the horizon in his windshield. Two hundred feet above the surface is about as low as is permitted to most pilots for any approach. Only a few certified professionals are allowed lower. At this "decision height," the pilot must be VFR. He must see the runway or the lights that beckon him to it, or he must pour the coals to the engine, climb back into the murk, and try again, or go elsewhere to land.

There are many fascinating sights to be seen from the air, but for many pilots the most thrilling remains the approach end of that long concrete ribbon that emerges out of the fog or appears suddenly as the plane drops through the bottom of the cloud deck. The runway lined up perfectly in his sight—its approach end growing larger, rising, as it seems, to touch the wheels—confirms his mastery of his instruments, a mastery that comes only through obedience to them.

An instrument approach is a triumph not only of the science of electronics and of man's ability to adapt to a different environment, but also of his ability to master both worlds of flight despite an abrupt passage from one to another.

And abrupt it is. The pilot may climb to altitude through a thick overcast, fly through it unerringly to his destination and descend again, seeing nothing but uniform whiteness. Until he breaks out underneath, several hundred feet above ground and perhaps only a half-mile from touchdown, he sees neither sky, ground, horizon, nor the airport he is approaching, not even in his mind's eye.

For it is only the novice who translates his needles and dials to a tilted horizon, too much ground, or too much sky in the windshield. It is the beginner who forms from the raw data of his instruments the mental images of the earth and his plane's relationship to it. Instruments speak a foreign language and the student must first translate into his native language before understanding the foreign tongue.

Sooner or later, he learns to *think* in that other language. Sooner or later, he discards that middle step. He need not translate. He no longer needs the crutch of that mental picture of his plane in space. The outside no longer matters. All that matters are his needles and dials. Directly and without translation the instruments shout their commands, and directly he obeys. The messages need not be processed. Only when his needles are where he wants them will he be at peace in his world of instruments.

Only then will he be ready to fly when even the birds are walking.

V

The Invincible Foe

It is six o'clock on a gray, rainy November morning and I am dialing the number of the New Orleans flight service station, My wife, Isabel, and I have planned to be in downtown Dallas by 11 A.M. and it is important that we keep the appointment. Planning a trip means figuring backward. An eleven o'clock appointment means landing at Dallas's Love Field at 10 A.M., which allows time for the rental of a car, the trip into town, and parking. Landing at 10 A.M. means a 7:30 A.M. takeoff for the two-and-a-half-hour flight. A 7:30 A.M. takeoff means leaving the house at 6:30 A.M. to allow for the drive to the airport and a preflight inspection of the two-engine Beech Baron, which I have flown to Dallas about a dozen times before.

There is one-half hour, then, to decide whether I take the Baron, as I have on all but one of these trips we have had to make over the last two years, or whether I cop out to the dreary weather and leave it all to Delta Airlines, as I did one nasty morning. To catch Delta's nine o'clock one-hour flight to Love, where the liners landed at that time, we must leave home at 7:30 A.M. If I opt for Delta, I can relax, forget about the weather, and spend an hour and a half reading or sleeping. But I do not want to fly Delta, I want to take the Baron.

Why do I fret so much? It would be simpler to take the commercial airline. I try to point out to myself various reasons why it would be better to take the Baron if I can. None of them make any sense. There really aren't any. I just like to fly the plane. Remarkably, so does my wife, who has come a long way from the days when she trembled at the thought. She likes the convenience and the privacy, and keeping her own schedule. She likes driving up to the plane and walking out of it to the small waiting room and the personal attention wholly lacking at the giant terminal on the other side of the field. The extra hour and a half en route is not too important. She will read, sleep, or needlepoint. The weather doesn't concern her. That's my problem. If I decide to go, then there is nothing to worry about, for if there were, I would not go.

It is very rare that I decide not to go. The Baron is a high-performance twin-engine plane with good radio equipment and instruments, and I relish the opportunity to use them. When visibility is good and skies unblemished I feel cheated. I have lost a chance to fly instruments. But with the clouds, sometimes, come other problems that are hard to handle, and combinations of problems that can be impossible to handle in a light plane.

Thunderstorms are one of those problems, ice is another. Low ceilings that would not ordinarily be a problem become a critical factor if the possibility of icing in clouds must be considered. An overcast with tops to 8,000 to 10,000 feet or higher, a welcome challenge when it hides only the view of the earth and sky, can become a nightmare when there is reason to think it may hide embedded thunderstorms.

On this gray, rainy November morning in New Orleans, I know the weather is clear in Dallas—windy, but cold and clear. But somewhere between Dallas and New Orleans there is a cold front. Exactly where depends on which weather briefer you happen to talk to, or what weather report you look at. There are terminal forecasts issued at major terminals every six hours for a twelve-hour period, and an area forecast issued every twelve hours for a twenty-four-hour period. Or is it the other way around? I can never remember, but it doesn't matter because it is not the forecast weather that interests you, but the actual weather when you are ready to go. Frequently, there is no similarity. The best you get on "current" weather is a sequence report giving you the weather at an exact moment, namely, five minutes before each hour, at an exact place, namely, an FAA weather station.

What is happening between weather stations or what has happened since the last sequence is anybody's guess, unless you get a special reports of severe weather, known as a "Sigmet," or one of not-quite-so-severe weather, known as an "Airmet."

Radar reports provide the best information about thunderstorms. Weather radar can see thunderstorms in progress. Unfortunately, it cannot tell you where one will start building in the next hour, or in the next five minutes. Weather radar tells you nothing about ice. Sometimes the various reports are in hopeless conflict.

Most often the weather is not much of a problem. There is a lot more good weather than bad. On rare occasions, the weather is clearly unflyable and the decision is simple. You do not go, at least not in a light plane. A solid line of thunderstorms with tops to 40,000 feet or more across your path and preceding a fast-moving cold front too long to fly around, is one example of clearly unflyable weather. A thick stratus layer loaded with ice, too high to top and too low to stay beneath is another. Thick fog, reducing visibility below landing minimums and covering very large areas, including your destination, leaving no suitable alternative if the destination is closed, is another. Those are the easy cases.

This particular morning, it was not easy. Conditions for icing were good, but the clouds were in layers. Layers mean clear air between. Ice does not form in clear air, only in clouds. Layers are much better than one solid layer all the way up to 10,000 feet, which is as high as I care to go. There were thunderstorms this morning, but not a solid line. Despite the forecast for a squall line, the reports were mostly of scattered storms.

The voice of the weather briefer rattled off information like a well-prepared schoolboy reciting in class. Broken layer at 900 feet. A solid overcast at 2,000, one at 6,000 and one at 10,000. The freezing level was at 5,000 feet in New Orleans and gradually lowered until it met the surface somewhere in north-central Louisiana. Light rime icing in clouds was reported by other aircraft. There should be no trouble between layers, though, says the briefer.

No trouble for him, that is. "What is the height of the top of the 4,000-foot layer?" I ask. Naturally, he does not know, but it wouldn't matter if he did. His forecasts are not written in stone. The cloud layers will not stay as they are just for me. I am not going to assume that the layers will not expand to merge and lose me in a solid overcast without a retreat, or that new layers will not form around me.

There are thunderstorms along the route with tops to 50,000 feet, but so far this morning the storms are only scattered, no lines or clusters. It should be no problem, he says. No, not if I can see them. But if I am in clouds, and nobody can guarantee I won't be, they may be quite a problem indeed. The thunderstorms won't be a problem unless the sky where I need to go to avoid them is occupied by clouds that leave crunchy rime ice on the wings, windshield, antennas, and props.

The stomach muscles tighten. Instinct tells me to forget it and call Delta. Experience tells me I am influenced more by the murky gray of the New Orleans skies than I am by the cold analysis of the information I get from flight service. Sometimes your instincts can mislead. If the point of departure is bathed in bright sunshine, it is easy to read reports of marginal weather en route without serious concern. In good weather, some pilots think they can handle any kind of weather. This is dangerous thinking. In bad weather, another voice tells you to forget flying light planes altogether, since it begins to seem dangerous even in the sunshine.

Mentally, I shut out the sound of drizzle on the windowpane and think of the reports. I have been through this before. There is every reason to think that once we are off and flying I will be quite comfortable. There will be ample clear air to avoid all of the monsters that loom larger in the mind as the sound of the increasing rain intrudes on my private thoughts.

It may be foolish but I am not going to cop out now. Not yet. I am going to check the weather again before leaving home and again at the airport. I am going to wait and see. Even at the last minute, should the problems worsen, we will simply drive from Lakefront Airport to New Orleans International, about fifteen miles away, in time to catch the Delta flight.

But, just in case, I better make sure we have seats on Delta's big jet. I have to consider not only safety, but the consequences of a missed appointment if we should have to turn back, or make an unscheduled landing to avoid bad weather. If we take the

Baron, I can call from Lakefront and cancel the reservations. As I dial the number, I wonder if the airlines are having their own decisions to sweat out and if perhaps the weather is too much even for the jets.

A cheery female voice answers my call: "Delta Flight 40 departs New Orleans International, 9 A.M. CST and arrives at Love Field, Dallas, at 10:05. Complimentary breakfast served on board. May I make your reservations?"

I hate her. How does she know the plane is going to land at 10:05? Does she not know it is raining? Does she not know the skies are loaded with ice and that there are thunderstorms about? She can sit in her office with her cheery smile, but I bet the pilot is not so unconcerned.

He is, of course, and has a right to be. The airlines long ago abandoned the lower atmosphere, the rain, the embedded thunderstorms, the ice, and all the rest of it. They took to the stratosphere above 90 percent of the world's weather, where the air is thin and jet engines efficient. The tops of the highest storms still protrude above the flight levels of the big jets, but they have the speed to get around the worst of the clusters in time enough to make it all worthwhile. No clouds are thick enough to hide an embedded thunderstorm from the eyes of their on-board radar and they have electrically warmed surfaces that can deal with all but the severest icing.

The big jets could take a shot at landing in Dallas no matter how thick the ground fog. It is always worth the chance that the fog will lift a little to allow the landing. And if it does not, there is no problem. The range of these monsters is such that they divert from Dallas to Houston, or Oklahoma City, or Nashville, or just about anywhere else to wait for conditions to improve.

So I tell the lady at Delta that she can make my reservations. I do not tell her that I hope to cancel shortly. I do not tell her that I'd rather take my own plane, that I only use their airline as a last resort, that I cannot stand her complimentary breakfast.

We made the flight that day to Dallas in the Baron. It was interesting, but uneventful; there was no ice, and there were no thunderstorms. I was in and out of clouds and there was some rain and a little turbulence. I have never understood much about ice and why, under the same apparent circumstances, it forms sometimes but not at other times. The temperature at 8,000 feet that day was right around freezing. I was in clouds quite a bit. According to all the literature, these are supposed to be ideal conditions for icing. But sometimes it happens and sometimes it does not.

Thunderstorms? Even if there had been a few lurking around the airway, I could have gone around. I was never in clouds long enough to worry about running into an embedded storm. Somewhere, about two-thirds of the way, we were out of the clouds and into the turbulent but clear air that follows the front.

Was all the agonizing unnecessary? Do I worry too much? No, it was not unnecessary and I do not worry too much. If you fly light planes, agonizing can be avoided in only one or two ways. First, you can assume, as some do, that you can handle any kind of weather, and if you planned to go, you go. The number of such fools is proportionately low to the pilot population in general and the death rate of such fools proportionately high. I do not want to die in a light-plane accident because, among other reasons, I do not want the boys in the coffee shop talking about me and shaking their heads. I certainly do not want to take anyone with me if I do "buy the farm," as the pilots say. Second, you can treat flying as a fair-weather sport only to be undertaken in clear skies, avoid all challenge, and get only occasional use of the machine. I do not want to do that either.

So I continue agonizing (on maybe 10 percent of my flights) over whether the weather is flyable. A few times I have canceled a flight and have been very glad to have done so.

I remember one trip to New York's La Guardia Field on Eastern Airlines. My plane was a twin-engine plane built by Piper, the Apache, which is not as powerful and as fast as the Baron, but a good plane. The entire East Coast was covered in white that day. From 30,000 feet, there is no way to guess the height of the smooth white layer, but from the briefing I had received in New Orleans before canceling it was probably quite high—maybe 11,000 feet—and I probably would have been in it for a long time. There was possibly light snow over a good part of the area, as had been forecast.

Safely ensconced in my plush seat, I looked and wondered. Should I have flown it? As we descended through the layer for the approach to La Guardia, the whiteness around us darkened, indicating a layer thick enough to keep out most of the sunshine. I heard the gear go down and I stared intently through the window. What I was looking for was that first glimpse of the ground, a glimpse that would give me an idea of the height of the overcast above it.

I could see the snow flurries blowing around us in the murk. That first glimpse was one of the tops of houses, partially covered with fresh snow, and of cars that appeared not too many feet below us. They appeared in my view for only a few seconds, followed by the fence on the airport boundary and the open brownish field of the airport, lightly decked in white. It seemed like no more than a few seconds from the moment we broke out to the moment we touched down.

We were, obviously, very low indeed and quite close to the field before seeing daylight. When we left the terminal to hail a cab it was bitter cold. As we crossed the Triboro Bridge, the city was obscured by fog. From Fifth Avenue, the tops of the highest buildings were not visible. I said to myself, "No way."

Had I been stubborn enough to insist on flying the Apache, we would undoubtedly have been waylaid at some airport in Virginia or thereabouts, where the cloud cover seemed to start, waiting for the weather to improve. Perhaps we would have left the Apache and taken an airline flight from there. Perhaps fate and the weather would have caused me to land at a burg where we would have needed a bus to make connections with a New York flight. Perhaps it would have meant changing planes or taking a milk run.

Whatever it would have meant, I could not have taken a chance on flying that length of time in icing conditions with no way out, short of descending to within several hundred feet of the ground. When it is well below freezing at the surface, there is a good possibility that the ice picked up in flight will stay with you all the way down. Ice does not form only on the wings—it will coat the windshield and prevent you from seeing things that, at low altitudes, you really ought to be seeing, such as tall towers, hills and, finally, the airport and the runway you are trying to land on.

There was no cause for regret or second guessing that day. My plane was where it belonged—tied down at the Lakefront Airport in New Orleans.

I don't always guess right. I remember on at least one other occasion looking at the fleecy broken clouds below me as I reclined in my airliner perch and said to myself that I could have done it. It would have been easy and a lot more enjoyable. But the regrets don't last long. Every private pilot has heard, and most believe, the adage, or some variation of it, that it is better to be on the ground and wish you were flying, than to be flying and wish that you were on the ground.

I have never made a mistake in the other direction, though I guess it could happen. I don't mean a mistake that would place me in a predicament from which there is no escape—I would never knowingly chance such an occurrence. I will chance meeting unflyable weather providing there is at least one sure escape route, whether below or behind or elsewhere. But I certainly could make a mistake that would prevent me from reaching my destination, a mistake that would cause me to say, "We're going back" or, "We land here and take the airline or a bus."

It happens. Discreet pilots sometimes have to leave their planes along the way and take commercial flights—a "real airplane," as some people say. They do this because sometimes it is dangerous to continue and because sometimes it is not worth the trouble. Sometimes they make it all the way to the destination, but find they cannot fly back. All such cases mean another trip to pick up the plane.

This is another circumstance that seems to place the light plane where the airlines were in the thirties. If you remember air travel in the thirties, or have read about it, you will understand the comparison. To fly in the thirties was a mark of distinction—and wealth. The speed of the plane was unbelievable—170–180 mph—about what the light planes do today. But you never could be sure of getting where you were going. There were maintenance delays, there was bad weather. If the early airliners had to land somewhere along the way, the airlines put you up in a hotel, or bought you a train ticket the rest of the way. Airline travel was an adventure. You never knew exactly when, or how, you would arrive. But at least someone else made the arrangements for you, and you did not have to go back to pick up your airplane.

Still, it is not quite fair to say that general aviation has not advanced in many respects. It has in some areas kept pace with airline flying. The airlines in the thirties, for instance, in addition to all the other problems, had cumbersome navigational equipment, low-frequency radio direction finders and four-course aural radio ranges, long antiquated by even the simplest high-frequency omnis in the least sophisticated light planes of the present.

Another sign of progress that reminds the light-plane pilot that he has advanced from the stone age is the surveillance radar monitored by the ground controllers who simultaneously talk to the pilot on an instrument flight plan and follow him on their radarscope. A vast network of radar covers practically every square mile east of the Mississippi and much of it west of the river.

The primary job of a man watching the scope is to keep planes from running into each other. But from time to time a controller is called upon to tell a lost pilot where he is and how to get where he wants to go—or where he needs to go before his fuel runs out.

To many pilots, radar network serves an even more important function. The remarkable radarscopes pick up not only airplanes and mountains, but also liquid and solid water, both of which abound in those towering terrors known as thunderstorms. It is not their job to point out these insidious monsters to the pilot, and their radar is tuned to a gain that is best suited to pick up planes and least suited to pick up thunderstorms. Nonetheless, the controllers often do pick up thunderstorms and, often, they do tell us about it.

It is a comforting thing to hear a voice wafting through the dark cabin on a moonless night, saying, "Zero One Tango, I show an area of precipitation at twelve o'clock about five miles. Would you like radar assistance around the area?"

Even in broad daylight, you cannot always tell these things, for as often as not, on a hot summer afternoon, one of these colossi hides another, and even when one storm is not hidden by its sister, the surrounding haze does the job.

More than once, I have stumbled into a valley of giants partially hidden in the haze and precipitation and wildly guessed at where they were and which was the best way to pass them, the pass that would permit them the fewest swats at me as I ran the gauntlet. It is a soothing voice indeed, in such circumstances, that says, "Zero One Tango, a heading of Zero Four Zero would appear to keep you out of the worst of it" or "Zero One Tango, I think you should be out of the precipitation in another two miles" or "I see a clear area to the right."

But, it is easy to rely too much on this voice from below. It is too much like that firm voice of authority that the child in us always yearns for in a pinch, to hand us on a platter the simple, straightforward solution to a complicated problem. Whatever it is in us that craves that voice of unquestionable accuracy and authority, it works overtime in the sky. To believe in such things, in the sky as on the ground, invites trouble.

Those who ride as passengers in light planes, and who listen to the seemingly omniscient voice from afar that fills the cabin, are too easily lulled. Surprisingly, so are some pilots. They sometimes envision the man below and his marvelous radar as scrupulously plotting the birth and death of every cloud in the sky, and, they assume that his purpose in life is to convey immediately to every pilot the exact location of every puff that forms.

I remember, in particular, one complacent passenger who was jolted from his reverie as we experienced the blows from the innards of a moderate summer-afternoon buildup. He demanded with a mixture of surprise and chagrin to know whether or not the controller had given me advance warning of that cloud.

Such confidence is touching, but undeserved. Severe and

often extreme turbulence precedes and exists within a growing storm. Only when growth has reached a certain advanced level, almost a state of maturity, does the vaporous moisture within those violent, alternating up-and-down drafts condense and become liquid. Only when it becomes liquid can it be seen on radar, which cannot see turbulence. It sees liquid or solid moisture—it sees precipitation.

The radar controller will tell you that he sees an area of light or strong precipitation. From the intensity of precipitation, you can get an idea of the turbulence. If ground radar sees no precipitation, do not believe that you cannot yet stumble into wild turbulence, turbulence that can throw you out of control. Such turbulence can exist in a large buildup that may not show up on the radarscope.

The life of the average thunderstorm is short but violent. Some have been known to last as long as twelve hours, but the average storm is only about an hour and a half.

This means that the tall, dark, ominous cloud up ahead may be just what it looks like, a growing thunderstorm, despite the assurance of the man on the ground that "I am not painting anything on my scope." Fly into it if you wish. There may be not only wild turbulence when you do, but precipitation and worse turbulence by the time you fly out the other side.

It is eerie. Sometimes the man on the ground can see it when you can't, and it is comforting; but, sometimes you can see it and he can't, and it is disconcerting, sometimes even frightening. You see this big, dark area ahead and you call this all-knowing voice in the box. And he says, "I am not showing anything." But there it is, and as you approach, it gets darker and it's boiling, so you tell the man on the ground what you see, but he's not perturbed. He assures you, as fathers assure children that there is no bogeyman in the bedroom. He says planes have been flying through that area from both directions and have not reported turbulence, but "deviate at will."

I decide to deviate, but there is too much of it. From my position, it looks like I couldn't get around that storm if I flew all day. I fly toward the lightest spot but very soon I am being thrown all over the sky.

I plod on through. It is not comfortable, but I can handle it. I see no reason to turn back. I want to get home and the man on the ground says it's safe. Except that now, inexplicably, he tells me that I am heading for the worst part of it and should turn right 270 degrees to a heading of 90 degrees and that he will get me through a lighter area.

Worst part of it? Worst part of what? A minute ago radar didn't see anything. Turn right to 90 degrees from my southerly heading? Why not left? It would be much shorter. Perhaps there is a strong cell ahead and to my left, and he wants to work me around it. All of this maneuvering to avoid weather that according to a radar report a few minutes ago didn't exist. It makes you wonder. Even when you are being tracked by radar, can a storm build right around you, and show nothing at all on radar until too late—until you are suddenly out of control?

Out of control—that is the whole problem. The danger from the rains, the hail, and certainly from lightning, is secondary. Turbulence is the real danger. The danger is not the precipitation the radar sees but the turbulence it's blind to. Updrafts at 5,000 to 6,000 feet per minute. Downdrafts of 3,000 feet per minute immediately adjacent. What radar doesn't see can put stress on any plane sufficient to tear it in two.

There is all kinds of advice about what to do when caught, despite all precuations, in a thunderstorm. Fly the artificial horizon; do not worry about rate of climb or descent. Do not fool with the power setting. Slow before entering the storm to a maneuvering speed, one which results, when the plane is subjected to excessive G forces, in a stall, rather than structural damage. You can always recover from a stall, or so they say.

But I wonder. Can you really recover when you are subjected to forces that could raise your airspeed dangerously while you do so? There is one school of thought that says very skillful flying can survive the worst storm. Another school says the worst cell of a storm can destroy any plane, no matter how skillful the pilot. I have no personal experience, but I have more faith in the second school.

It is a tremendous help to have a ground radar system that can get you around most storms, even those you cannot see, but ground radar is far from foolproof. No one with any knowledge of radar systems even claims that it is. There are times when you do not even want to listen to the wise man on the ground. Not many times, but some. There are times when you wish he would just go away.

Like the night I flew home from Dallas in the Beech Baron. The trip that morning had been simple, but the drive to Love Field after dinner resembled piloting a submarine. It poured, it thundered, it lightninged. I sat in the comfortable pilot's lounge provided by the fixed-base operator, and called from time to time to see what the thunderstorms were doing. Which way were they moving? How long before I could take off?

The rain slackened. It always does. But the lightning! It flashed across the southern sky like the flashes of an automatic weapon. Not much noise—just a lot of light, flashing light. I remembered all the chapters in the books, and all the magazine articles I had read about lightning. In the entire history of aviation, there are only two known cases of planes being knocked down by lightning. In most cases, the books say, it just leaves a little hole, about the size of a half-dollar, in the plane's skin. Sometimes it knocks out radio equipment or causes the compass to go crazy. It can temporarily blind the pilot. But the occurrences are rare and the consequences seldom serious.

So? So, when the briefer tells me that the storms have moved off to the south and that the airway to the east is clear, I take my emotions, meaning my fear, lock them in a box, and rely on the solid information. I file my flight plan and advise my wife that we are taking off.

I am told to maintain 3,000 feet until I get further clearance to my assigned cruising altitude of 7,000 feet. This seems to be routine coming out of Dallas. Only tonight the ceiling is just above 3,000 feet and the lightning isn't just flashing—it is like someone flicking the light on and off in a room you are sitting in. The lightning does not appear to come from any particular place. It simply lights up the entire ceiling right above you for a few seconds at a time. You can read a book in the plane's cabin. It is as though you have finally come to the place where they make the lightning.

After fifteen minutes or so comes the dreaded command of the guy on the ground: "Climb to and maintain 7,000 feet."

I do not want to climb. The lightning is bad enough down here. I do not feel like climbing into the ceiling anymore than I feel like putting my head inside a fluorescent bulb. I try to remember whether I have really heard, or read, that flying inside a cloud while lightning is at work is more dangerous, or if I only think I have.

I tell the controller I do not want to climb, there is a lot of lightning. He cannot hear me very well though I hear him fine. I have to repeat three times. Finally he understands. He is disgusted. He tells me to turn right heading 120 degrees. I do not want to turn right heading 120 degrees because that brings me closer to where I know the lightning is coming from, though it seems to be coming from nowhere in particular. I am quite certain it will keep me a safe enough distance from the turbulence of the thunderstorm, but I do not want to turn any closer to the source of all that light.

I will not turn right and I say so, but now the controller cannot hear me. I hear him tell me to turn right or to climb, but he does not hear my refusals.

Finally, a friendly voice from a Cessna breaks in. I do not know exactly where he is, but he can hear me and he can talk to and be heard by the Dallas departure controller.

"Zero One Tango says he cannot turn right because it would put him right in the thunderstorm," says my friend in the Cessna. It is nice of him to help, but he could at least get the story straight. I did not say anything about the thunderstorm. I am worried about the lightning.

The departure controller is angry. Controllers rarely show anger on the airwaves, but this one is really annoyed. "Tell Zero One Tango that is no reason to disregard instructions. There's traffic coming against him and he's creating a dangerous situation. There may be clouds, but I can see there's no precipitation on a course of 120 degrees. Tell him to follow instructions."

Up yours, buddy! Down here below the clouds visibility is good. I can see fine, and I am not going to run into any other airplanes. I know you can see where the precipitation is on that radarscope of yours, but you cannot see the lightning. I can and I'm scared. I am not going to climb and I am not going to turn right.

I continue in silence. In time, I call the Fort Worth Center Controller, the man responsible for monitoring the next phase of the flight. He is more sensible. He tells me to climb to 7,000 feet *when I feel it is safe to do so.* In time, the lightning stops. The clouds break up and the moon is visible. From 7,000 feet, the lights of cities can be seen for many miles. The rest of the trip is routine.

The vagaries of the weather make life interesting. If we had nothing but good weather, life in general, and flying in particular, would not be nearly so intriguing. It is the weather that renders every trip different from every other trip, even over the same route.

In the little instructing I have done, I have told each student at least once that a light-plane pilot does not tell his passengers that he is going to such and such a place on such and such a day. He says, rather, I am going if the weather is okay. What weather is okay depends on each pilot. But for every pilot, there has to be some weather that is not okay. A pilot who thinks he can fly in all weather is not safe in any weather. The passenger ought to know that ahead of time, because if he *has* to get to a certain place at a certain time, he ought to call Delta, or Eastern, or Pan Am, or somebody—just in case.

VI

Roller-Skating on the Interstate

It is all well and good to speak of a different kind of flying, of flight in our own part of the sky separate from that used by the jets of commercial aviation. But we often leave from the same nesting place and sooner or later come down to the same place to roost. And no matter where they leave from or where they come to rest, the jets must invade our part of the sky to get to or from their own.

And because of this inescapable fact, we are often plugged into the same ground equipment, talk to the same controllers, and show up on the same radar screens. Often we get the same type of clearances in the same specialized language. It couldn't be otherwise. It wouldn't do for either world of flight to ignore the other.

Whether we can stay in our own cocoon and isolate ourselves from the progress as well as the headaches and complexities of the last thirty years by avoiding contact with "the system," depends on many things. Pure, unfettered pilot preference is one of them. The length and altitude of the flight is another. The weather is another—probably the most crucial—factor.

For all our complaining about all the rules and restrictions, a pilot in this country can still, in halfway decent weather, take off in a light plane without filing any kind of flight plan and fly, with a few exceptions, the length and breadth of the land. He needs permission from no one if he has a license. Nor need he tell anyone where, when or even if he is going. I do not believe that there is another country in the world in which this is so. I know that it is not true of another country in this hemisphere.

From any of thousands of landing fields and small airports scattered across the United States that have no government-operated control tower, a pilot may legally take off and land without a radio. For despite the complaints about excessive regulations, there is no requirement that an airplane even have a radio. There is only a requirement that the pilot maintain radio contact with ground controllers in certain relatively small areas. If he avoids those areas, he doesn't have to talk to anybody at all. And if he does take off or land at an airport that has a government-operated control tower, he need only maintain radio contact with the tower controller within five miles of the airport.

He can fly the limit of his aircraft range, whatever it may be, 600, 800, or 1,000 miles, and never talk to anyone at all if that is his preference—*if* he obeys all the *ifs*. He must avoid areas restricted for military or other reasons, and busy terminal areas. If crossing within five miles of the center of any airport with a government-operated control tower, he must remain at 3,000 feet or more above the ground. He must stay away from clouds and have at least three miles visibility. He must stay below certain altitudes that are usually beyond his plane's capability anyway.

Even the restriction of the busy terminal control areas is not absolute. Many of them have VFR corridors—a tube of airspace of a certain width and height through which light planes can fly without radio contact.

Pilots who complain about growing restrictions on use of the airspace might do well to shift their glance on occasion to the vast spaces that are unrestricted. Those who complain about how much instrumentation they now need for certain types of flying ought to look at how little they need for most of it.

Government-operated flight service stations, located at or near many airports, large and small, are there for the convenience of the pilots for the filing of VFR or IFR flight plans, to open the VFR plans once in flight, to check weather, to ask for certain information, or to make a position report if they wish. There is no *requirement* that they be used in flight at all. The chief advantage to opening a VFR flight plan is that someone will come looking for you if you do not show up at your destination when you should.

At many small fields without control towers there are government-contracted privately operated radio facilities known as "unicom." They furnish airport weather and traffic information on request. There is no requirement that anyone talk to them either.

And if the pilot does wish to intrude upon restricted air space, an airport traffic area, a terminal control area, or to take off and land at a controlled airport, at all but the busiest terminals, the radio communication is minimal and simple.

But all of this freedom depends upon reasonably decent weather. It depends upon staying out of clouds. The pilot can fly around them, under them or over them, keeping certain minimum distances. Sometimes it is a nuisance to dodge clouds. Sometimes it is inconvenient, time-consuming and uneconomical. At times it is extremely difficult and at times, impossible. Reasonable assurance that it will not be difficult or impossible to avoid clouds exists on many days for short distances or short periods of time—less frequently for longer ones.

When the weather is not good enough to fly by VFR, if the pilot wants to fly at all he must file and fly IFR. The weather doesn't have to be unfit for VFR for the pilot to make an IFR flight. He can file and receive an IFR clearance in any kind of weather. But when he does, he gives up the freedom to go when, where, and how he pleases and the right to go in silence. The IFR flight plan must be cleared and he must follow the plan.

An IFR clearance is a clearance to follow a certain route at a certain altitude. It matters not at all to the air-traffic controller whether the route takes you through clear skies, growing cumulus, heavy stratus, or scattered cotton. The ground controller expects to see you on his radar screen on the route that was assigned, or to hear you confirm your position on that route if there is no radar coverage at any particular time or place. He expects confirmation by radar, if the plane is equipped to report that way automatically, or verbal confirmation if it is not, that you are at the altitude that air-traffic control has assigned.

Clouds are so prevalent, dodging them such a nuisance, and weather forecasts so tentative, that peace of mind on all but relatively few flights comes only with an IFR clearance. If you start VFR and conditions deteriorate, if the weather goes sour, it is possible to file and get a clearance in the air. But it can result in delays, and it can be awkward. It is easier to get a clearance while sitting on the ground waiting for takeoff than while trying to fly the plane.

In a very real sense, the real freedom of flight lies in IFR. It is the freedom to fly in a straight line without dodging harmless clouds. But it comes at a price. You are no longer subject to the tyranny of merging temperature and dew point, but you are plugged into "the system." Flying IFR means a clearance, continual radio contact to confirm your adherence to that clearance or to receive a new or amended clearance, or to deviate as instructed or as permitted.

It means being led by the hand. You are told by each successive ground controller whom to contact next and on what frequency, what altitude to fly, when to start your descent for the approach, and when you may begin the landing approach itself.

It is in this system that there are the most points of contact between the two parts of the sky, the two worlds of flight. The two are joined by umbilical cords to the same parent throughout the entire flight, not only during takeoff and arrival at the roosting place. That cord consists of radio and transponder contact. The controller hears you on radio, and by means of the on-board transponder identifies you as a blip on his radar screen.

The system is equipped to handle traffic of all types, just as the Interstate highway is able to handle heavy trucks, autos, bicycles, and even people on roller skates if they are so inclined.

With the exception of the inevitable snafu, the system works remarkably well, guiding, separating, and bringing home to busy terminals heavy transports, jumbo jets, business jets, high-powered single- and multi-engine propeller planes and single-engine trainers. From the pilots it sometimes provokes silent admiration, and sometimes, audible irritation. To the passengers who listen to the steady flow of radio chatter between the ground and the pilots of their own and other airplanes, it is sometimes annoying, distracting, or frightening; other times or to other passengers, informative, fascinating, or amusing.

It starts with ground control at the airport of departure. The ground controller clears the pilot to the active runway for takeoff. The pilot of an IFR flight, whether of an airline jet or a four-seat single-engine job, receives his clearance either from the ground controller before taxiing or, at the busiest terminals, on a separate frequency assigned to a clearance delivery. His flight plans and request for clearance have been filed by the pilot before getting into the airplane.

The clearance shows the route to be flown, the heading to be flown following takeoff, usually one designed to intercept that route, the altitude to be maintained, the transponder code to "squawk," namely, a four-digit number to set up on the face on the instrument, and the frequency of the departure controller to contact after takeoff. Clearances are read back by the pilot to insure that they are understood. When ready for takeoff, the radio is switched to the tower frequency for the takeoff clearance.

The problems and the incongruities that result from the mix of huge jets and small propeller planes begin even before takeoff. At certain times at certain fields, if you look closely at the planes lining up, you are apt to see a four-seat single-engine high-wing pygmy sandwiched between two 100-seat, three- or four-engine swept-wing Goliaths. If you do not look closely, you are apt to miss it. Only the bright colors of a tiny insect amid the almost solid-silver skin of the big birds attract the attention of the casual observer. It is the same at all of the larger airports in Dallas, Atlanta, Washington, New York, Denver, Miami, or other cities of similar size. Your taxi instructions are apt to be as follows: "Taxi to runway 9 right; fall in behind the DC-10 taxiing west on Golf [the designation of the taxiway]." You fall in line behind the DC-10. Another DC-10, or a 707, or a 747, calls for taxi instructions and is told to "fall in behind the Baron."

So there you are. You could almost taxi underneath the one in front of you and no one but you would probably know. More ominously, the guy behind could roll over you, and no one at all would know.

If I am taking off at the wrong time from the wrong airport, there is likely to be a long delay. I may be fourteenth in line. I try to avoid that, but when you travel you like to leave early and early morning is the busy time on the active runway. I try to get out even earlier, but we don't always make it, what with traffic delays in town, bad service at the restaurant, or preflighting the airplane.

But sometimes because of my size I get a break. Sometimes as I wait on a taxiway that parallels the runway the controller will call and say "Zero One Tango, if you can cut across the grass, I can get you off now." He is telling me that if I cut across the grass between the taxiway and the runway, I will not have to wait my turn in line to take off. He will clear me out of turn.

Why? Maybe because he knows I don't need all that runway and that it is pointless for me to wait in line with the ones who do. Maybe he is nervous about my getting run over by the guy behind me. Maybe he just thinks I look out of place and destroy the aesthetic allure of the line of sleek jets. If he were not so busy, I would ask.

Contact after takeoff with the departure controller, who sits in a radar room at the same or a nearby airport, is usually acknowledged by an instruction to "ident." This obliges the pilot to press a button on his transponder that brightens his display on the ground radar screen. The departure controller has now confirmed that the blip he is looking at is the plane he is talking to. This is followed by the cheering news of "Radar contact," and usually then by, "Turn right [or left] heading 280 degrees [or whatever]. Join Victor 40 [which is the designation of an airway]." Or the pilot may be instructed to maintain a certain heading, or "vector," to avoid traffic, following which he will be given a heading back to the airway and told to "resume normal navigation."

About twenty-five miles from the airport the controller instructs the pilot to contact the air route traffic control (ARTC) center on a designated frequency. "Contact Houston Center now on 125.6. Have a good flight," is a likely transmission.

These centers are strategically located throughout the country. There are seventeen of them: Houston, Jacksonville, Atlanta, Washington, Denver, and Miami are a few. The call to the center controller is brief: "Houston Center, Cessna 1253 Hotel [for H] climbing to maintain 7,000," for example. Altitude is all the pilot needs to give, and if you're equipped with encoding altimeter, not even that. The center controller is watching the flight on radar and knows the plane's position more accurately than the pilot does. The center controller may ask for an "ident" to confirm what he has on his screen.

The ARTC centers have been part of the system for a long time. I do not know how long, but since well before radar became a fixture at all of them as it is today. Not until the late fifties did the government begin to blanket the nation with radar coverage. Prior to that time, centers kept tabs on the positions of planes on IFR flights by means of position reports from the planes themselves. The pilots reported the time over certain radio-defined fixes or locations, gave an estimate to the next fix, and confirmed their altitudes. Since ARTC knew the direction of flight it was a "simple" matter of mathematics and plotting to give pilots the proper instruction to avoid having two of them try to occupy the same space at the same time, or even to come dangerously close. Position reports are still required for planes not in positive radar contact, which happens sometimes.

Altitude clearances were also somewhat different in the fifties. It was assumed that while not in clouds, there was not much danger of collision or of two pilots' not seeing each other. Clearance might be for a specific altitude or it might be for a specific number of feet above the overcast. This latter type of clearance depended upon a very fickle factor, the location of clouds at any particular time, and was an uncertain quantity.

But an occurrence on June 30th, 1956, hastened the elimination of this type of clearance and the advent of the radar coverage we have today.

On that day a United Airline DC-7 was proceeding eastbound from the West Coast along the Grand Canyon. Its clearance was for 21,000 feet. A Lockheed Constellation of Trans World

Airlines was proceeding northwest, also across the canyon, The clearance for the Constellation was 1,000 feet above the overcast.

The overcast that day was 20,000 feet. The crew of the DC-7 did spot the Constellation, but too late to avoid a collision. Pieces of one of the liners decked with streaks of paint from the other were removed from various locations within the canyon, as were most of the bodies of that plane's passengers. Most of the wreckage and bodies from the other liner were inaccessible and were not recovered for many years. Fifty-eight persons were aboard the DC-7; seventy aboard the Constellation. There were no survivors from either plane. It was the worst civil air disaster until that time in United States aviation history.

The Civil Aviation Authority's and congressional investigations, as well as a public outcry, resulted in the radar network that exists today. Sooner or later, with the explosive growth of commercial aviation, such a network was inevitable.

Today these centers control all IFR flights in their areas by means of remote outlets. As the flight moves across the area of a particular center, it passes from one segment to another, each guarded by a different remote outlet. It is tracked by that outlet's radar and as the pilot communicates on a designated frequency with the controller responsible for flights through that segment it guards, he is instructed by the controller to contact "center" on the frequency guarded by the next outlet and is picked up by its radar.

He is now talking to a different controller, though this new controller sits in the same radar room in the center, probably right next to and rubbing shoulders with the previous one.

These remote outlets are necessary because both radar and VHF radio operate on line of sight. The center is responsible for an area with dimensions of hundreds of miles, but direct contact with planes, particualrly in the lower altitudes, is not possible at such distances.

So our flight that has taken off from an airport in the area controlled by the Houston center is "handed off" from one Houston controller to another and from one frequency to another as it comes within and then leaves a segment guarded by a different remote outlet. The last Houston controller, depending on the direction of the flight, will say "Cessna 1253 Tango, contact Fort Worth Center now on 124.1." Only now will the pilot talk to someone in a different city in a different little room.

In recent years, flights at the lower altitudes are often handed off to approach controllers as pilots fly toward or near various terminals at which there's an approach-control facility. It is just a matter of distributing the work load. The procedure is the same.

The flight is handed off from one controller to another, and from one center to another as it moves across the country. The conversation is repetitive. It is routine. The pilot soons knows what the controller is going to say before he says it.

He is instructed by the departure controller to contact an en route controller at the control center on a designated frequency. His first call is: "Houston Center, Cessna 1253 Tango is with you at 6,000." Altitude is all he needs to give. Houston answers: "Cessna 1253T, Houston, ident." The pilot may say "53T" or he may press the button and say nothing. "Radar contact," responds the Houston controller, "Houston Altimeter 29.97 [or whatever]." The pilot turns a knob on his altimeter to correct for nonstandard atmospheric pressure so that when his altimeter says 6,000 feet he will really be at 6,000 feet or reasonably close to it.

And that may be all. It may be the last word exchanged between those two gentlemen until fifteen, twenty, or twenty-five minutes later, when the controller says, "53T, contact Houston Center now on 126.7. So long." And the whole routine is repeated. Only the numbers, and maybe the accent of the controller, are different.

But there may be other chatter. If so, it is likely to be: "Five three Tango you have traffic at two o'clock, five miles, headed southwest at 7,000" or, "Fifty-three Tango traffic at nine o'clock, westbound, altitude unknown." The "altitude unknown" means it is VFR traffic and not in contact with the controller. If he were in contact, the controller would know his altitude.

Sometimes the word from the controller is, "Five three

Tango, turn right headed 210 degrees for vectors around traffic,'' meaning that you and another craft on IFR are likely to pass within less than the minimum allowable distance of three miles. Sometimes the vectors are for help in getting around weather. Sometimes there is an amendment to the clearance.

The radio chatter is almost always predictable. Almost always unpredictable is the reaction of passengers to it, particularly of those new to flying light planes. Most planes have switches that permit the pilot to cut out the radio from the overhead speaker and to receive only in his own earphones. Sometimes with new passengers, I will leave the cabin speaker on as I get taxi instruction, clearance for takeoff, and communication with the departure controller, at least through the first radar contact. Then I usually switch it into the earphones, believing the monotony of the repetition is nothing, in time, but a distraction. A passenger making his first light plane excursion often asks what has happened to the radio. When I explain, he sometimes want me to switch back to the speaker. Veteran passengers sometimes make the same request.

Why do they want to listen? There is no point in asking. The passengers probably do not know themselves. I think, particularly when the sight of the ground is obscured or cut off completely, it is a feeling of security, a lifeline to the familiar world. I think they like to know that someone down there is looking out for us.

It is not confidence in the pilot that relaxes some passengers, it is confidence in ground-based radar. They expect to hear, from time to time, ''Radar contact,'' as we are passed from one controller to another, and they are uneasy when they do not. The routine ''Radar contact lost,'' which inevitably occurs for short periods, disturbs the equilibrium of some passengers. I was once quite certain that one companion believed the plane was supported in flight by radar and that malfunction of the ground radar would cause us to fall from the sky.

On the occasion of revealing to my wife my plans to fly from New Orleans across the Gulf of Mexico to the Yucatán Peninsula, her concern was not the long expanse of water, or the

600 miles to Merida without a runway beneath us, or the fact that for much of the flight we would be out of range of VHF navigation facilities, relying only on the less accurate low frequency beacon. Her concern was aroused only when I had to inform her that we would be out of range of the friendly radar men.

There are voices of other heros to soothe the nerves too. The passenger hears other pilots talking to the controller. The voice from Piper 7340V may not add much interest to the flight for most passengers but the voice from Braniff Flight 402 certainly will. I sense that it seems to give passengers a certain tranquility, sometimes a certain pride, and sometimes even a little thrill to know that they fly the same system and that their pilot talks over the same airwaves to the same controllers as do these hoary old captains who command the leviathans of the skies.

And you can always tell those old captains. Even when you pay no attention to the identification, you can tell them. The voice is professional. It is two octaves deeper than the voices from the Beechcrafts, the Mooneys, the Cessnas, and the Pipers. His is the voice of the surgeon in the room filled with interns; the voice of the old judge amid the law clerks. There is a casual, devil-may-care timbre to his shorthand phraseology that says: "I have been this way a thousand times before." When he talks to the controller, you can often tell that two old friends are nodding, even if the phraseology is entirely formal and proper. It has the sound of two men who pass each other on the same corner at about the same time every day: "Good morning, Fort Worth, Delta 901 with you at flight level 33." "Delta 33 roger, good morning. How about an ident and the altimeter this morning is 30.02." When I am obliged to talk, I feel like an intruder.

Sometimes they provide more than entertaining listening. They can see much weather on the deck from their crow's nest. And they don't mind passing it along nor do they mind relaying position reports for us to distant stations that we cannot reach. This is particularly true of flights over long stretches of water. And sometimes the relay comes the other way.

I am flying north from Tampico, Mexico, along the Gulf, bound for Corpus Christi. I have not been able to contact the Mexico City center to get my IFR clearance for the flight into Texas as I had been instructed. I continue northward, increasingly far from Mexico City. I will call Brownsville, Texas, for it before crossing the border, but I would prefer to have it now. The weather is such that I need it.

A paternal voice breaks in on the Mexico City frequency: "Zero One Tango, this is Delta Flight 402, over."

"Zero One Tango, go ahead, Delta."

"Zero One Tango, Mexico Center has been trying to raise you for a while, but I guess you're out of range at your altitude. They want a Brownsville estimate and your route of flight out of Brownville."

"Brownsville estimate" means the time we think we'll get there. I give him an estimate without doing a lot of calculating, figuring it will be at least as close as most Delta arrivals and I give him my route to Corpus Christi. He repeats my information verbatim to Mexico City. I cannot hear Mexico's response, but a minute or so later he tells me that Mexico says Brownsville has cleared me as requested. No big thing, perhaps, but the effort was appreciated and I tell him. "You bet," are his parting words. It is comforting to know that these giants can and do take the time to help.

The monotony, if it is monotonous, ends with the approach. Transmissions en route may often be substantially the same for hours. Transmissions when a pilot is finally handed off to the approach controller at his destination are not so predictable. The particular approach procedure in use at the destination airport, the runway to be used, weather and traffic conditions at the field are all unknowns as a rule until fifteen or twenty minutes before landing. The instructions, particularly at the larger terminals, come faster; traffic is denser. En route we see little traffic nearby; in the terminal area we often get close looks at other airborne planes. The instructions now are not only for horizontal flight, but we are brought down in steps from cruise altitude: "Turn left heading 040 degrees, maintain 4,000." Before we reach 4,000, the voice may order: "Continue your descent to 2,000, report reaching,'' meaning he wants to know when we are level at 2,000 feet.

Radio work aside, even on the VFR flight, even on the flights to small fields, there is still a little bit of drama in the approach to the airport and the landing. I do not know why. But it is there and it is perceived by almost everyone aboard. Few passengers continue reading or talking during the last phase of the descent. Even in good weather details of the ground that for several hours have been out of sight, now come into view. There may be the intriguing vista of the central part of the destination city or the geometric pattern of homes and swimming pools in the suburbs.

When the clouds hang close to the ground there is the tenseness of the approach on instruments. All eyes wait for the first glimpse of the earth. On more than one occasion a passenger has signaled his relief from tension by applauding as the wheels touch the ground. I remember a whole cabinload of passengers in a commercial jet liner doing the same thing as the craft touched the fog shrouded runway at Jackson, Mississippi, just a few hundred feet below the overcast.

And the approach is the place at which the liners burrow through ''our'' sky. You have seen good views of some of them shortly after takeoff, but after that you see only specks far above, or more often, only the contrails. Not until the approach do you see them again. Not until the approach do we share the same part of the sky.

When you see them approach and descend through your level as you loaf along at 6,000 or 9,000 feet, it is an interesting, sometimes a thrilling sight, and poses few traffic problems. A call from a ground controller that you are being overtaken by a ''707 descending through 8,000, will pass you on your right,'' causes all heads to turn. You seem to be moving backward as the monster sinks past your level and drops away. Sometimes, once safely a thousand feet below you, it will begin a gentle turn across your path.

I remember flying southeast toward New Orleans from Oklahoma City one late afternoon at 7,000 feet. The route runs about thirty or forty miles east of Dallas's Love Field. At the time, Love was a major airline terminal; now primarily a general-aviation airport. Ahead and to my left, a couple of thousand feet below, a jet liner was proceeding toward my flight path. His speed was such that he was obviously going to cross a couple of miles ahead.

I watched the ship's graceful lines until my attention was attracted to another behemoth a few miles behind him and at the same altitude. He was going to pass closer. I riveted my attention on him because this one was going to afford a better look, but as he passed from left to right, ahead of me, still another caught my eye. This one was going to pass right below me. As I watched that streamlined hulk, seemingly close enough to touch, I saw a fourth member of the family far off to the left, but the parade was over. He passed far behind me.

This was obviously an initial approach point for Love Field. I heard none of this on my radio, since these birds were with Dallas Approach. I was with the Fort Worth center, so it was a silent performance.

Such invasions of the lower skies by these inhabitants of the stratosphere and their proximity to the slow-moving natives pose no serious problems to pilots or controllers. My presence at the line-up presented no danger. It was simply a sudden, unexpected, awe-inspiring spectacle. I felt as though I had stumbled into a den of elephants in the midst of a strange ritual.

But the approach of the jets and light planes at the same time to the same airport does sometimes create problems. The problem is that jets are fast and general aviation planes are slow. Some are slower than others, but compared to the jets they are all slow. At our altitudes, most often less than 10,000 feet, there is a speed limit, but that limit of 250 knots, 288 mph, is twice as fast as the top speed of many light planes, and almost three times the speed of most trainers. In airport traffic areas, which means under 3,000 feet within five miles of the airport center, the top speed is slightly less, but not enough to make a difference to a 100 mph trainer. And even light planes have to slow substantially from their own normal crusing speed as they approach the field in order to prepare for landing.

The controllers usually want the little birds to keep their speed up, especially during an approach to a large terminal, if it is very early or late in the day. "Cessna 59T, keep up your speed on final as long as possible." "Piper 34 Poppa, let's try and give me a hundred knots on final." He sometimes tries to motivate us: "I have a DC-9 at six o'clock, three miles."

To complicate matters, controllers sometimes like to keep us high as long as possible to keep radar contact. This is particularly true when the approach radar facility is at a nearby but different airport from the one of destination. I have had them bring me practically to the airport boundary at 5,000 feet above ground before turning me loose to the tower controller. Only a dive bomber could get down at high speeds without much maneuvering to lose altitude. Rapid loss of altitude and high speed do not go together if you want to keep the plane in one piece. To "keep up your speed," as the controllers like, requires a long, flat approach. A steep approach means low speed to cover less forward distance at a particular rate of sink.

To complicate matters just a little further, the manufacturers and mechanics warn against powering back at high speeds. The engine will cool down too quickly, they say; you must keep some power in until you flare for landing. Keeping the power in slows the descent, causes a longer approach, and from the altitude at which the controllers turn you loose, it can take you right over and beyond the airport.

You can't keep your speed up enough to avoid complicating their lives under most circumstances and as a rule you cannot give them anywhere near as much help with their traffic as they'd like. Most light-plane pilots try to avoid the big terminals, at least at the busiest times. But sometimes it just isn't feasible. I suppose anything is possible. We could take the airlines or a bus. But we pay taxes too.

One late fall afternoon I approached Washington National Airport from Atlanta in a Piper Apache with three passengers. It wasn't absolutely essential to go to National, but Dulles is a long way from town, as are the general-aviation airports. I intended to get in earlier, but I didn't. I caught the late afternoon traffic. I was at 5,000 feet above an overcast that had a base about 2,000 feet above the city.

The approach controller is vectoring an endless stream of airliners to a point about five miles up the Potomac River for a visual approach known as the Potomac River approach. The planes follow the river as it meanders southeast through the city toward Chesapeake Bay. Then, as they approach National Airport, the planes turn right onto the southeast runway.

My turn comes soon: "Piper 4429 Poppa," he says, "turn left headed 330 degrees, vector for the Potomac River approach." I acknowledge. I am crossing over the city and there are breaks in the overcast, revealing enticing glimpses of the capital city. I admire the sights but at the same time I wonder what I am going to do to the long line of jets that willl be sent down the river behind me.

While I am wondering, the mind of the ground controller has apparently not been idle. "Two-nine P," he says, "do you have sight of the ground?" I do and I tell him so.

"If you can spiral down where you are to 1,000 feet, I can bring you directly in on Runway 21." I am just north of the airport at 5,000 feet, just east of the restricted airspace over the Pentagon. I see what he wants me to do, and it will save me a lot of flying.

There are two possible reasons for this offer. First, perhaps he realizes that we have probably been flying for a long time, that we are tired, and that we would like to get down and settled in our hotel before it gets too late. Or second, he is worried that my 100-knot speed down the river will play hell with his traffic. Either way it is an attractive offer.

I do have some hesitation. I was kind of small for my age in high school, but in my junior year I went out for varsity football anyway. As I was running with the other candidates, the coach unceremoniously yelled as he pointed at me, "Son, you're too little. Go play with the junior team this year." Now here he was again.

It is a minor matter; I accept his offer. I throttle back; I dump the gear and flaps and I start a 45-degree-bank descending turn. One of the passengers says something that signals apprehension, but I want to get down; I really do not want to rumba down the Potomac with those jets. As I roll past 2,000 feet the controller says to stop my descent at 1,000 feet and roll out on a heading of south.

He says it as if it were easy. I wonder whether any of those liners ever did a fancy approach like this.

It really is easy but it takes a little practice. If someone says to chew gum rapidly and move your hands in a circle and then says keep chewing but stop moving your hands, unless you are careful you will stop chewing at the same time you stop moving your hands. As I reach 1,000 feet and stop the descent, automatically I roll out of the turn even though I am not heading south. It occurs to me later I might have rolled out headed west, which would have brought me over the Pentagon.

Whatever the reason, the controller's reaction is swift, if restrained. "South, 29 Poppa. Roll out south. South is 180 degrees." I turn to a heading of 180 degrees as the controller continues with a steady stream of instructions to other planes. As I roll level at 180 degrees and head south he tells me, "That's right, 29 Poppa, you're doing fine. Do you see runway 21 right ahead of you?" There is just the slightest hint of sarcasm in his voice. I knew he didn't like me the first time I heard him. I land on runway 21, a short, narrow strip, suitable for light planes only, as the jets scream onto runway 18 from their descent down the Potomac.

That time my short legs worked to my advantage and get me in line ahead of the big ones. My approach to New York's La Guardia late one afternoon resulted in a different procedure to avoid a potential traffic problem. The controller decided to just put me on the sidelines for a bit while waiting for a lull in the traffic. But that too resulted in an unexpected dividend.

I do not make a habit of showing up in the late afternoon at busy terminals. But this flight to New York along the eastern ridge of the Appalachians was my first brush with "wave effect." An unusually strong crosswind coming across the mountains resulted in severe downdrafts. I knew the wind would be there. But a crosswind, no matter how strong, causes little decrease in ground speed. I had not counted on the extensive and severe wave effect, however. I was constantly climbing at a slow speed, just to hold altitude. I was tired and at first did not appreciate the controller's vector to the west as I approached the tip of Manhattan. Just as I wondered how far west he would send me I was told to do 360-degree turns to the left at my present position "for spacing" until further instructions.

As I dipped my wing to the left, there was revealed to me and my delighted passengers Lady Liberty in all of her glory. Many times I had practiced turns about a point while east of New Orleans, using a road intersection, a highway sign, or a bush. Never did I expect to use the Statue of Liberty as a pylon. As a boy of sixteen I had seen her once from the Staten Island ferry. In later years I got a glimpse on occasion from Battery Park. I had never made the trip to the island where she stands. After our fortuitous two circles around before being called in to land at La Guardia, such a trip would be an anticlimax.

Not always are conditions such that we can be spiraled down to another runway or put safely out of the way for a while, doing circles. Sometimes weather conditions do not permit it. But even under the worst conditions there are usually ways to juggle the traffic.

"Zero One T," says Dallas approach, "ceiling is 700 overcast. When you break clear can you switch to 31 right. I have fast traffic at the outer marker."

I am coming down the glide scope of the ILS in solid instrument weather on the approach to runway 31 left at Dallas' Love Field. What the controller is asking is that I sidestep, after breaking clear, over to a parallel runway about one-half mile to my right so that the fast traffic behind me does not have to hold. To "hold" means to waste time by flying a race-track type pattern at a certain point while I complete the approach and get out of their way.

"I'll let you know when I break out," I answer. I would be glad to do it, but there is no way to know that the 700 feet is accurate until I get there. I am still a few hundred feet higher. I would not want him to clear the jet behind me until I am actually in visual contact, for there is no safe way to line up with 31 right until I see it.

The 700 feet is accurate. Less than a minute after his request I tell the approach controller I am clear and that I will accept 31 right.

"Zero One Tango, roger, turn right, intercept 31 right approach course. Contact tower now 118.1. Thanks for your cooperation."

And when even that option is not available?

"Eastern 307, hold at the outer marker," I hear as I fly the approach to Birmingham Municipal Airport. "I have a little fellow coming down the ILS and he won't be out of the way in time." The "little fellow" is me.

Such delays to scheduled liners are rare. I feel bad about them when they occur, since the jets waste a lot of fuel when delayed. But in Birmingham there is no place else to go.

The purpose of it all is to keep planes from colliding in midair. It works fairly well. Out of roughly ten million domestic civil flights a year, airline, corporate, business, pleasure, and training flights, there will be in an average year approximately thirty midair collisions. Most of these occur in the vicinity of the airport, in good weather, and involve planes that are not on instrument flight plans. Surprisingly, less than half of all collisions involve fatalities.

The entire subject is a serious one and is treated that way by most pilots. I take it, perhaps, a little more serious than most, for my own moment of truth was a midair collision that came very early in my flying career, shortly after it was resumed, following a nine-year layoff.

I was flying a rented Cessna 172, a four-seat, 150 hp high-wing craft, and returning to New Orleans Lakefront Airport after a short flight along the Mississippi Gulf Coast. It was a clear day and traffic in the vicinity of the airport was heavy.

I am still not completely sure about what happened, despite the investigation and lawsuit that followed.

Approaching the airport, I turned to fly downwind, paralleling the active runway. The path took me well out over Lake Pontchartrain. A student with only twenty-three hours and a few hours of solo logged was concluding a series of touch-and-go landings in a 100 hp high-wing trainer. Communications between him and the tower had not been very frequent. The tower personnel were not sure who he was as they saw him on a collision course with my plane as I turned to base leg, a path 90 degrees to the final approach.

There are many blind spots in all airplanes—especially those with high wings. One drawback to the high-wing is the inability of its pilot to see into his turn. Drop the wing just slightly and the entire field of vision is blocked to that side. It was from that side, my left, as I banked and turned to the left, that the trainer approached.

There are other blind spots in a high-wing plane. You cannot see to the side above you, just as in a low-wing craft you cannot see to the side below you. This particular high-wing trainer was below my plane and the pilot undoubtedly could not see me. Through a combination of circumstances, we apparently wound up in each other's blind spot.

I am sure he saw me first as I continued my turn, which brought me across his path from his right. I must assume that. I cannot know for sure, because he did not survive the collision. But when I saw him, he was in a steep left bank, as though trying to evade my plane.

The tower warned me of a plane off to my left and as I lifted my wing, I saw him. The arc of his steep left turn brought the underbelly of his trainer beneath my plane, where it was sliced by the low portion of my prop. I saw him no more than a few seconds before the collision, time enough perhaps to react had I a clear idea of what reaction might have avoided the collision. But to me, collision seemed inevitable, or at least in the hands of fate. Planes do not react as instantaneously as cars do to sudden movements of the control and I resisted the immediate impulse to turn and thereby lower a wing in the path of the plane that was obviously passing below me. I stayed straight and level.

The collision sounded like two garbage can tops being struck together next to your ear. The other pilot was killed when his plane, sliced in two, fell into Lake Pontchartrain. My plane, with a bent prop blade, a cracked main spar, dented wing strut, and other minor damage, shuddered and shook, but, with no loss of thrust or performance, was safely landed.

The accident occurred where and when most midair collisions occur—in good weather, in the vicinity of the airport. The investigation that followed resulted in no administrative action against me, and the lawsuit against me was dismissed before trial when the heirs of the deceased pilot settled with the government.

Nonetheless, I have relived those few moments repeatedly and will always wonder whether something I could have done in those last few seconds would have saved the other pilot. I will never resolve it, nor will I ever resolve the matter of whether any attempt to avoid the collision would have resulted in the destruction of both planes instead of one. This is something that I cannot think through to a conclusion. Aboard my plane were three of my four children. They were physically unscathed and the psychological impact was overcome with time. At ages six, ten, and eleven, they felt the enormity of the tragedy that did occur, as well as the one that might have occurred, less than I did.

Well-meaning friends have told me, only half jokingly, that I must be statistically one of the safest pilots aloft, for no one, probably, has ever been in two midair collisions. I do not feel that way. The first one is history. A new one is as likely to happen to me as to anyone else.

Pilots are not a very sentimental lot. Nor are controllers. There is a lot of bellyaching by airline pilots, general aviation pilots, and controllers about one another. Their gripes appear in the letters to the editors and sometimes the editorials of flying magazines and the conversation around hangars and airport snack bars. They rarely admit what is a fact nonetheless: there is a lot of camaraderie among pilots and between pilots and controllers. It is not expressed nor does it need to be. It is implicit in every communication. The purpose of almost every transmission is the same: to avoid having two planes run into each other. The purpose of the remaining transmissions is equally praiseworthy.

This singleness of purpose against the specter of midair collision or other dangers inherent to flight is the source of the silent bond. It is sensed by the nonpilot and these repetitious communications are often a sense of security to him. And it is undoubtedly this that causes many passengers to tap the pilot on the shoulder and say, "Would you mind fixing the radio so I can hear it?"

VII

Plane and Pilot—A Mutual Misunderstanding

It is a fact of life often denied by pilots, but a fact nonetheless, that flying light planes is potentially a dangerous pastime. Pilots will tell you that it is all a matter of knowing what you are doing and being careful. If you take all the necessary precautions and use good judgment, they say, it is safer than driving a car.

They may be right. Except that the ability to exercise a high degree of care over a very long period of time is itself questionable. A pilot's ability to exercise extreme caution and good judgment always seems to be under attack by two insidious foes: flying too much and flying too little. Fly too much and flying gets routine and you get careless. Fly too little and you get rusty. Both of these conditions can cause the most obvious types of pilot errors, the types that cause the boys back at the coffee shops and Coke machines to shake their heads in wonder. Implicit in their behavior is the unspoken assurance that "it could never happen to me," but the boys are wrong. It could happen to anyone. There is only one way to avoid all risk of pilot error: leave the plane tied down at the airport.

From the moment the pilot opens the throttle and tears down the runway for takeoff, there is a risk. Perhaps it is not an unacceptable risk, but there is an element of risk in private flying not present in commercial air travel or in driving automobiles. That element derives from the fact that the inherent dangers of flight are minimized only by a professional approach and a self-discipline that few are capable of on a sustained basis during what is essentially a leisure activity.

Perhaps, for those who can exercise professionalism and self-discipline in leisure activities, private flying is as safe as driving. On most flights the pilot feels that there is no risk because *he* is careful, has taken all precautions, and will use good judgment.

This is the exact opposite, however, of professionalism, which implies constant doubting, questioning, and skepticism.

Flying can be as safe as driving, but not for the pilot who thinks it is. It is as safe only for the pilot who says, at least to himself, that flying is potentially dangerous, that—unless he seeks out and learns to minimize what dangers exist—that graceful bird in the hangar will turn on him and kill him at the first opportunity. If the pilot accepts the dangers of flying as an eternal and relentless foe, then flying may be safer then driving; but if the pilot believes that flight in a light plane is inherently as safe as driving, then it is not. The risk has gone up—call it a Catch-22, if you will.

There are too many things involved in safe flying to justify a smug attitude. The catalogue of obvious pilot-error accidents is endless. Experienced pilots have taken off without checking for gas, have run out of gas, and have had to crash land. They have checked the gas and not put the cap back on securely, and the wind has quickly siphoned off the gas in flight. Pilots have neglected to untie tie-down ropes of low-wing planes and have taken off with the rope trailing in the breeze and wondered at the degraded performance of the plane. One pilot of a large plane taxied out for takeoff with a piece of concrete block dragging behind him. Doors have not been properly latched and have come open in flight. This is usually not a matter of great moment, depending on the type of plane, the pilot's presence of mind, and other conditions, but a factor nonetheless in more than one fatal crash.

Pilots have killed themselves taking off, or trying to take off, with control locks still in place. It happens despite the fact that new pilots are taught that one of the first things to be checked outside of the plane, before starting, is the freedom of movement of the control surfaces; and taught too that one of the last things to be checked, inside the cabin, right before takeoff, is the freedom of movement of the controls themselves.

More than one case is on record of a crash resulting from a reversal of the aileron control. The pilot banks left upon moving the controls to the right, instead of vice versa, which would be normal. This is an error in installation following repair work or painting that would have been easily discovered by watching the ailerons while moving their controls on the ground before takeoff. Either the pilot forgets to check them or, more likely, checks them mechanically, without really looking or thinking.

Sometimes pilots have even taken off without removing the pitot-tube cover. The pitot tube itself is a small metal tube extending, usually, from beneath the wing, and is the source of airflow for the airspeed indicator—quite an important instrument. Failure to remove the protective cover is especially difficult to understand, for attached to it is a red cloth on which is usually stenciled in white lettering: "Remove before flight." It would seem that no one with an ounce of intelligence would attempt to take off without removing the clearly marked cover, which I guess is how the ground controller felt as he radioed to me one day as I taxied out. He said that there appeared to be a long red cloth hanging underneath my wing and did I want it there.

That was not my only lapse. Among the relatively few sins listed above, other examples come readily to mind. These include one tie-down rope trailing from the plane, one taxi for takeoff without realizing that the rudder lock was still on, and more unlocked doors than I can remember. These derelictions do not embarrass me as much as you might expect. They have happened to pros with many more thousands of hours than I.

Pure carelessness. Everyone knows better. But there are other dangers more likely to overtake the inexperienced and less likely to vex the pros—though these dangers sometimes inexplicably trouble pros also. The real danger of mishandling the plane occurs sometimes through carelessness, but often through ignorance. Sometimes an unwary pilot is done in by a danger in which he was totally untutored. These dangers are not the supernatural monsters and demons that ancient mariners feared. They are the natural laws of aerodynamics, but the fate they hold in store for the unwary is just as frightening and much more real.

There are, for example, a number of pilots each year who collide with the ground because they do not understand that there is an angle of attack beyond which they enter into a strange world of "reverse command."

There is, theoretically, for every plane one speed that forms the boundary of this seemingly unnatural realm of "reverse command." In a climb it is the speed below which you climb at a lower rate rather than a higher one. At any speed above that magic number, while at a constant power setting, the slower your speed the more feet you climb each minute. Once you get below that speed, however, that is no longer true. From that point on, the slower you go, by pointing the nose higher, the fewer feet per minute you climb, for you are now in the realm of reverse command. Or, as the engineers say, you are on the back side of the power curve. In a climb, this speed is known as the "maximum-rate-of-climb speed."

The term "maximum rate of climb" is self-defining, but some words and terms are used so often that the users hear only the sound and forget the meaning. I have heard pilots say that their planes have a maximum rate of climb of so many feet a minute, but that they can climb somewhat faster by slowing by five or ten miles per hour.

Maximum-rate-of-climb speed is not the speed at which you climb at the sharpest angle—that speed is a few miles slower. Maximum-rate-of-climb speed is the speed at which you climb the most feet per minute.

In a descent, this boundary-line speed is called the "speed of minimum sink." This is not the speed at which you glide the farthest—that speed is a little faster. The speed of minimum sink is simply the speed at which you sink the fewest feet per minute. Go slower than that magic speed and you sink faster; go faster and you also sink faster.

In level flight, that boundary-line speed is the speed at which you can maintain level flight with the lowest possible gas consumption, and thereby stay in the air the longest amount of time, not the speed at which you can fly the longest distance, which is somewhat higher. Nor is it the slowest speed at which the plane can fly. It can fly slower. But it takes more power and more gas to maintain a lower speed, not less power and less gas.

This boundary-line speed is theoretically the same for all three elements of flight: climbs, descents, and level flight. Actually, the speed, the magic boundary, differs slightly among the three elements because of the effect of the propeller, but not enough to matter. It also varies slightly with altitude, temperature, and weight.

But understanding the theory is more important than knowing the precise numbers. The pilot does not need to know the exact location of the boundary. He needs to know that there is a boundary. If he knows that this other realm of flight exists, he will know when he has reached it.

Such is the upside-down domain of "reverse command," into which unknowing pilots stumble from time to time. To the pilot who knows the territory, it is not a dangerous place to be. To flee there in fear, to wander there through neglect, or to be unaware of its existence, is a potential disaster.

Inexperienced and improperly instructed pilots approaching for landings will try from time to time to stretch their glide by bringing the nose higher and higher, oblivious to airspeed, and to the fact that the plane is suddenly sinking faster. They react against the fast sink with more back pressure, encouraged by the fact that they *momentarily* reduce the sink rate, until the plane smacks into the ground short of the runway. The descent could, and should, have been stopped only with additional power.

Sometimes pilots purposely slow to uncommonly low speeds and "drag" it in with power. This is the only correct approach to a very short strip. The slower your speed on flaring, the less runway will be eaten up before the plane settles to the ground. But without power, at that low speed, the bird will mush right out from under you. A "mush" is what occurs when the sink cannot be stopped because of insufficient air speed and control response.

When the nose gets too high in a climb, and the rate of climb starts to fall off, there is no option. You cannot increase your climb with power because, in a climb, you are already using full power or something close to it. Go too slow and you can increase your rate of climb only by lowering the nose to gain speed! This is exactly the opposite response to that which becomes instinctive to the pilot during his initial training. Flight students are told about the power curve, but most often it is learned as something merely theoretical.

So, on occasion, pilots continue to land short of the runway or to clip a hill, rooftop, or telephone wire on climbout, desperately pointing the nose higher and higher. Sometimes it is the result of poor planning and ignorance. Those that survive usually blame the engine. It lost power, they say. Inspection and investigation often indicate otherwise. Often, it appears the pilots have gone in nose-high with their engines putting out full power, oblivious of the low airspeed and its consequences.

But it is in the emergency situation that the whole phenomenon assumes vital importance. And it is in the emergency situation that it apparently is most often forgotten. Too often the subject has not been brought home to the pilot during training with enough force for it to become second nature. This is unfortunate, because it is that second nature that saves us in emergencies, when the first nature, conscious thought, does not function too well. But none of us, regardless of training, can ever be sure it will work for us until the time comes.

Engine failure, total or partial, sometimes results in more damage, more injury or unnecessary fatalities because in the acute stress of the circumstances the pilots, according to investigation, apparently have ignored whatever they have learned about the relationship of speed to rate of sink. We read the reports of others' misfortunes and wonder how we would react under similar circumstances.

It is better to hit a fence or a ditch or to land in the trees with flying speed, belly first, and in control, than to stall, or worse, spin and drop like a rock, nose-first, even the last forty feet. Or so we are told and so we tell others.

Unfortunately there is no way to train for a real emergency. We can read and hope to absorb. We can practice and hope that proper use of the controls becomes instinctive. But there is no way in practice to simulate the conditions of a real emergency.

We could suddenly pull the power when a student is least expecting it. I suppose we could even conceal the cause of power loss, such as surreptitiously switching off the gas, and pretend to be as surprised as the student. I have never done it, and for many reasons, would consider it bad practice.

But even if we did, the simulation would fall short on two counts. First, the student knows the instructor will take the controls in a real emergency. And secondly, it would be foolhardy, almost suicidal, to extend such pretense to the place where it really counts—the last 100 feet before touchdown on whatever dirt road or open field may be available. It is the last desperate effort to avoid a ditch, a treetop or a fence that is apt to cause us to forget it all—the books, the lectures, everything.

So one continues to read of light-plane pilots, sometimes professionals, sometimes instructors, some with thousands of hours of flight time logged, who died in crash landings following fuel starvation or mechanical failure. One sometimes sees pictures of the wreckage planted nose-first in the earth, leading one to suspect a stall. Or it may have a smashed underbelly, leading one to suspect that it dropped in unnecessarily hard from unnecessarily high because of the same panicked incursion into the realm of reverse command.

But without the connivance of any emergency at all, some pilots still, according to accident reports, spin in on the final turn to the runway. To do this the pilot must be fond of approaching low and slow. Then he must skid the plane around the turn, unconsciously reluctant to bank sufficiently while that near the ground, or reluctant (those in high-wing planes) to block their view of the runway. There is danger in a flat turn at low speeds, especially when too low to recover from the stall and spin that can result from it. These pilots did not know, or never really absorbed the fact, that in a flat turn one wing, the one to the inside of the turn, flies more slowly than the other. At slow speeds, the slow wing may stall while the other, the outside wing, still flies. This is exactly what a spin is. The plane suddenly rotates wildly around its vertical axis because one wing is flying and the other is stalled. Newspaper reports generally say that witnesses observed the small plane "drop" from the sky as it approached to land. But planes do not drop without a reason.

If accident reports are to be believed, perhaps one of the most insidious causes of aerial catastrophe is the fact that planes perform according to the density of the air—better in high density, worse in low density. It is a circumstance not unrelated to the realm of reverse command, for it is one of the forces that drive us there. Because density of air decreases with altitude, many pilots equate the two and soon assume that density depends *only* on altitude and, others, even if they know better, assume this in their actions.

The takeoff run for a plane at a given weight under given wind conditions, for instance, depends on air density. Air density depends in turn on altitude above sea level and temperature. It depends on altitude because there is less atmospheric pressure on a given volume of air at a higher altitude than at a lower one. Atmospheric pressure is the weight of the total column of air from the ground all the way up. If we take off from a high-altitude airport there is less pressure from this column on the air through which we make our takeoff run and the air is consequently less dense. There are slight variations in this pressure from day to day, even from hour to hour, at the same location, but these variations are small and can usually be disregarded.

What cannot be disregarded however is the temperature. The effect on air density caused by the variance in temperature can be tremendous and can seldom be disregarded except on long runways in flat country, preferably at or not far above sea level.

So dramatic is the change in an airplane's peformance with a change in temperature that those who make the rules had to come up with a new name for it. Unfortunately, they may have compounded the problem by calling it "density altitude." They define density altitude as "altitude 'corrected' for atmospheric pressure and temperature." The unofficial literature compounds it further by explaining that density altitude is "how high the plane 'thinks' it is." In other words, say the writers, on a hot day the plane at 5,000 feet flies as if it is at 7,000 feet because, as pilots like to say, the plane "thinks" it is at 7,000 feet.

But if we look deeply into the plane's psyche, we will probably see that the plane does not really care how high it is. It pays no attention to its height above sea level in flight or to the elevation of the airport from which it takes off or to which it approaches to land. The plane cares only about the density of the air through which it moves and which it uses to burn fuel for power.

As a student it took a long time for me to get it through my head that density altitude has nothing to do with height above ground, but only with aircraft performance. As an instructor I have seen other students take just as long.

Stated in different terms, the plane and the pilot simply do not speak the same language. Instead of speaking of "density altitude" we might do better to speak of the "altitude density" of the air, which would at least emphasize the density and not the altitude.

The altitude, or the height above sea level, is told to the pilot by the altimeter, which really measures atmospheric pressure. Temperature does have an effect on the altimeter, but an entirely different effect from the one it has on air density and consequently aircraft performance. Except at extremes of temperature, the effect on the altimeter is not great and can be disregarded. The all-important fact is that the altimeter by itself does not tell us all we need to know about the performance of the plane and the effect on it of density altitude.

Short fields, fields at high altitudes, and high temperatures, singularly or in combination, are the traps for pilots who ignore density altitude and for their unfortunate passengers.

To avoid hitting fog-shrouded mountains, or to avoid the peaks at night, you need to know high you are above sea level. But to figure out whether your plane can climb fast enough to avoid hitting the ridge that you see looming across your path you need to know your density altitude, or, if you insist, how high the plane and its engine think they are. The ability of a plane to climb depends on the density of the air it flies in, which is all that the plane and its air-breathing engine "know."

In order to be able to talk at all about airplane performance, or density altitude, pilots and plane manufacturers have had to figure out some arbitrary set of conditions as a standard from which to measure. It means nothing at all to talk about how fast a plane climbs from sea level, or how long a runway it needs for takeoff if the airport is 2,000 feet high, or how fast it flies at 3,000 feet, except with reference to certain conditions of atmospheric pressure and, much more important, of temperature.

So the authorities had to select a "standard" set of conditions. When a pilot says his plane needs 1,200 feet of runway to take off, that it climbs 900 feet per minute, or that it flies 165 mph at 8,000 feet with a certain power setting, he means, or should mean, that these facts are true under standard conditions. The conditions that have been selected as standard are atmospheric pressure producing 29.92 inches of mercury at sea level and a temperature of 59° Fahrenheit, or 20° Centigrade, at sea level. This "standard" temperature drops approximately 3½° Fahrenheit for every 1,000 feet above sea level. These figures are supposedly the average, or mesne, of the pressures and temperatures existing at most places at most times on earth, or at least a rough approximation.

Some places never see standard conditions for months on end; other places never see standard conditions at all.

Let us forget about standard pressure. The variation in total atmospheric weight, or pressure, at a given altitude based on non-standard conditions is small and does not make a great deal of difference. Let us speak only of temperature, which does.

On any summer afternoon in most of the Deep South and on many summer afternoons elsewhere, the temperature is closer to 89° or 99° Fahrenheit than 59°, so even if the airport is near sea level, the plane, in pilot's parlance, does not know it. It thinks it is at 3,000 feet and performs as it would at a 3,000-foot-high airport at standard temperature, about 49° Fahrenheit at that altitude, which is not as well as it performs at sea level with the temperature at 59°.

The trap for the unwary pilot is made even more treacherous by the fact that the so-called standard conditions are selected arbitrarily and are quite unrealistic. Although pilots know that performance is less at higher altitudes and at higher temperatures, pilots are not always conscious of the fact that the standard temperature itself decreases as the altitude increases. And the trap is that it is almost as likely to be 90°F. at Salt Lake

City, Utah, or Grand Junction, Colorado, both over 4,000 feet above sea level, as it is at Jackson, Mississippi, or Montgomery, Alabama, just a few hundred feet above sea level.

When the earth's surface is at 4,000 feet above sea level, it heats up the adjacent layer of air just as well as it does when it is at sea level. It may make sense to speak of standard temperature dropping 3½° for every thousand feet above the earth's surface. To speak of standard temperature at *ground* level being 14° less simply because it is 4,000 feet above *sea* level makes very little sense, except that it is a convenient, consistent, and simple formula to use—when you think it is necessary to use one at all.

Unfortunately, it is contrary to common experience and for that reason is ineffective. Too often there is nothing to drive home to the pilot that he needs to start using formulas.

I was in Cheyenne once when it was a crisp 60° on the ground, which in Cheyenne is 6,000 feet above sea level. "Standard temperature," I thought, without really thinking. I assumed that the plane would perform at least like the book said it would perform at 6,000 feet. I soon realized it would not. The density altitude was not 6,000 feet; it was about 7,300 feet. But because I was not wiping the sweat from my brow, nothing drove home to me the fact that my bird's performance would be crippled by the "heat." Only at 38° at Cheyenne would I get the performance at Cheyenne that the book that came with my plane told me I would get at 6,000 feet.

How many days between May and September does it dip to 38° in Cheyenne? Not many, according to the city's own tourist brochures. The problem does not end there. When the transient pilot passing through Cheyenne does wipe the sweat from his brow in 80° or 90° weather, he may, in his own mind, add distance for takeoff, usually the amount he needs to add when he feels the same heat in Chicago, which is at sea level. But he is off the mark. His plane does not "think" it is 2,000 feet higher than it really is as it does back home in Chicago. Now it thinks it is 3,000 feet higher than it really is because there is a bigger difference between 90° and 38°, which is standard temperature in Cheyenne, than there is between 90° and 59°, which is standard in Chicago. The plane thinks it is at 9,000 feet, in other words, rather than the 8,000 feet that the pilot may think. At those altitudes, light plane performance is poor, and the 1,000-foot difference is significant if the field is short.

For every 1,000 feet above sea level the plane thinks it needs an extra 10 to 15 percent of runway for takeoff. If there is not enough runway, it takes whatever is there, such as the airport fence and the parking lot beyond.

Not only do planes need more of a takeoff run at higher density altitudes, but they also climb at a slower rate. A light plane's best rate of climb is from sea level. As it climbs, the rate of climb drops off. It may rise from a sea-level airport for instance, at 1,200 feet a minute. As it climbs through 6,000 feet, the best rate of climb may be down to 600 feet a minute. At 10,000 feet, it may be down to 400 feet a minute. The "ceiling" of most light planes is somewhere around 18,000 feet. This ceiling is reckoned as the altitude where the rate of climb is down to 50 feet per minute. (All altitudes mentioned are density altitudes.)

So what does it all mean? If you look west from Denver, you will know what it means, for you see mountains that rise 5,000 to 9,000 feet and more above the great plain on which Denver sits. They rise suddenly without prior announcement of their presence by the foothills that usually precede a change in terrain from flat to rugged.

The plain itself is 5,000 feet above sea level. The fact that this indicates a need for a greater takeoff run is unimportant to the light-plane pilot in Denver even on a hot day, for the runways at Stapleton Airport are 10,000 feet in length. The fact that the plane climbs much more slowly is quite important, however, to the pilot whose route after takeoff is to the west.

The light-plane pilot crossing the Rockies west of Denver does not aim for the 14,000 foot peaks; he wants to cross at the lowest ridge in the area. But that itself happens to be at almost 12,000 feet.

As he climbs toward the west, the mountains look close, probably a lot closer than they really are, since visibility out west is often fifty miles or better. Will he make it? It looks to him that he will not. His nose is pointed somewhere below the ridge. So back he comes on the controls. Now his nose is pointed above the ridge, at least until he gets closer. He does not realize that his nose is pointed much higher than his path of flight. He is too intent on looking at the mountains to think of such theoretical things as angle of attack. He is too intent sometimes, despite the fact that up where the air is thin and the light plane is near the limit of its performance, the angle of attack is quite large. The nose may be pointed above the ridge, but the path of flight may take you right into it. Somewhere, the pilot reduces his speed, through continuing back pressure, to the point where he is beyond the best rate of climb. He is on the back side of the power curve and the more back pressure, and the slower he flies, the less his rate of climb. Slow enough and he will sink, mush, right into the ridge.

Such ignorance is rare, but not so rare as might be supposed. Even an uninformed pilot from the east will usually successfully traverse the terrain out west because the power of his plane allows performance to spare. Or, he will see the problem, if not the cause, and circle until he gains sufficient altitude. Or he will turn, and go back where he came from.

But more than one luckless and uninformed birdman from the lowlands has told FAA investigators that he crashed because his plane lost power. Investigation usually reveals that the pilot had all the power at 12,000 feet that he had a right to expect—which is not much.

Sometimes the pilot doesn't get that far. He never has to worry about clearing the peaks because he smacks into a hillside a short distance from the airport, or into the treetops right past the end of the runway. Denver may have 10,000-foot runways but many of the mountain airports do not. The 2,500-foot runway at the airport nestled in the hills 4,000 or 6,000 feet above sea level looks to the pilot as long as the 2,500-foot strip he is used to near sea level. As far as his plane is concerned, it is only half as long.

First of all, the engine, the kind used in most light planes, will, at 4,000 feet, develop less power, maybe only 80 percent of its rated power. Second, in that thin air, it takes a higher *ground* speed and, consequently, a longer takeoff run, to get up to the same *indicated* airspeed that is needed for takeoff.

Indicated airspeed? Ground speed? Yes. Because we insist upon speaking of airplane performance in terms of the altimeter, and because the altimeter fails to speak the language of the plane, giving by itself no indication of the real performance we can expect, one set of problems are created. The airspeed indicator, however, *does* speak the language of the plane, but uninformed or unthinking pilots sometimes do not understand that, and that creates another set of problems.

Pilots do not talk about speed in the abstract. They talk about ground speed, indicated airspeed, and true airspeed. These are the minimum three terms in the pilot's vocabulary when he discusses speed.

Ground speed refers only to the time it takes to travel between two points on the ground, and it is determined by the true airspeed and the wind. The speed and direction of the wind, except for momentary changes caused by gusts, do not affect the flying characteristics of the plane in the slightest degree. Whether there is a 50-knot headwind, a 50-knot tailwind, or a crosswind, makes no difference to the plane.

The speed that does affect the flight characteristics of the plane is the airspeed. The dial that sits in front of the pilot and that feeds him information crucial to the safe handling of the plane is the airspeed indicator. A plane may stall below a given airspeed under given circumstances, no matter how high, because of a tailwind, the ground speed may be. The plane may suffer structural damage if it gets above a certain airspeed, no matter how low, because of a headwind, ground speed may be. The force of the air entering a pitot tube, the forward-facing opening mounted outside the plane, moves the levers and dials of the airspeed indicator. It measures the speed of the plane relative to the air in which it moves. Only when the wind is still, which is practically never, will the airspeed indicator give a direct indication, with a readily calculable correction, of ground speed.

The force of the air that is measured is determined not only by the speed of the plane through the air but also by the density of that air. The less dense the air, the less force it will exert at the same speed on the levers and dials. So, at the same speed through the air, the higher you are and the hotter the weather, the lower your airspeed indication. The exact difference between this *indicated* airspeed and the *true* airspeed, which is airspeed corrected for altitude and temperature, can be calculated on little computers that can be found in every pilot's back pocket, hanging from his belt, or nestled in his flight bag.

Once again, the crucial term is not altitude, but density altitude—not how high the plane really is, but, using 59°F. and 29.92 inches of mercury as standard, how high does the plane act as if it is? The hand computer will show that for every 1,000 feet of density altitude the plane will actually be going about 1.5 percent faster than the airspeed indicator says the plane is going. This is what the pilots use as a rule of thumb. At 7,000 feet and an outside-air temperature of 80°F., the density altitude might be 10,000 feet. If the airspeed indicator says 150, the pilot must add 15 percent of 150 to determine the true airspeed of 172. So the plane relative to the air is moving 172 mph. The 150 mph on the dials is not a true reading.

Let us return to the man from the lowlands, who is ready to take off on his 2,500-foot strip, nestled in the hills 4,000 feet above sea level. Let us assume the temperature is standard, which at 4,000 feet is about 47°F. At sea level, he has to accelerate his plane to an indicated airspeed of 70 mph to take off. But at 4,000 feet, when his needle hits 70, he is really doing about 75 mph. He is doing 70—that is, a true airspeed of 70—when his airspeed indicator gets to about 66 mph.

Shouldn't the plane take off at 66? Shouldn't the plane take off when it gets to a certain speed, rather than when the dial reaches a certain number? The plane doesn't read the airspeed indicator. The plane certainly doesn't, but it does respond to the same fluctuation in air density as the pitot tube and the airspeed indicator it is connected to. In other words, the airspeed indicator speaks the language of the airplane. It feels that same speed that the plane feels. The altimeter reports to the pilot how high he really is above sea level, not how high the plane feels as if it is. The airspeed indicator, however, does not report how fast the plane really moves through the air, but how fast both it and the plane feel as if they are moving.

The plane cannot read the instruments, but it is just as sensitive to the reduced density of the air as the airspeed mechanism. One must move through the air at 4,000 feet at a speed of 75 mph to obtain the same effect produced by denser air at sea level at 70 mph. The reduction in lift caused by the thinness of the air is exactly proportionate to the reduction in the dynamic force of the air as it moves through the pitot tube. What counts as far as the plane's performance is concerned is not true airspeed, but indicated airspeed. Consequently, the pilot must accelerate to a true airspeed, which in a no-wind condition is the same as a ground speed of 75 mph. This is five mph faster at 4,000 feet than at sea level, and the pilot must accelerate with only, approximately, 80 percent of his sea level power. Pitot tube, wing, and engine all feel the loss of air density.

What is the difference? The difference may be that between clearing treetops and hills or not doing so, between a plane on the wing and a hunk of twisted metal. The difference is plenty to the pilot who flies entirely by feel, and feels that he is going fast enough to fly. He sees the runway and adjacent objects moving beneath and past him at a certain familiar speed and tries to lift his plane off, just as he always does when the runway moves that fast beneath him.

He does not watch the airspeed indicator during the takeoff roll. He has made so many takeoffs, and knows his plane so well, that he knows exactly when he is moving at 70 mph. Or perhaps he does look, but thinks the plane flies by true rather than indicated airspeed.

Maybe our hypothetical pilot knows exactly how far he needs to roll to take off even under the worst conditions. To him the worst conditions mean simply no wind, or no wind and a hot day (taking off into the wind shortens the takeoff run as you start your run with some airspeed to your credit). But, our unknowing hypothetical pilot may not be prepared at all for the need for increased ground speed caused by the increased altitude of the airport. So he lifts his plane off when *he* feels it is ready to fly based on the ground speed that *he* is used to. It may lift off, but it will not climb.

There is a so-called ground effect, an increased lifting force of the dynamic air close to the ground, which gives the plane a slight additional lift. But it exists only within a relatively thin layer near the ground and the plane will fly at that low speed only within that layer. Before it can climb any farther, it must pick up additional speed. And it picks up additional speed only be accelerating in level flight, not by climbing. This means keeping the nose down.

With the trees at the other end of the runway coming up fast, this is not easy—it feels unnatural. More and more back pressure is often exerted unconsciously as the trees, or rising terrain, at the end of the runway grow larger and larger in the windshield. The plane rises only a foot or two if at all. Everything the pilot has learned, which may not be much to begin with, is now forgotten. He sees only the danger looming ahead and applies more back pressure.

The plane may rise a foot or two, but then it starts to sink, nose high. Too late to cut the engine and land. Too late to accelerate and climb. Too low to turn. The fate of the pilot and passengers are in the hands of dumb luck and the odds are against them.

This scene is re-enacted from time to time not only at high altitude airports, but at short fields at any altitude, especially on hot days, when density altitude is high—when the plane acts as if it is at a high-altitude airport even at sea level. These are days when the airplane, the engine, and the pitot tube all sense less-dense air, even though the pilot may not. Pilots used to taking off on 5,000 to 10,000 foot runways may pay little attention. To them, whether they get off in 1,200 feet, or 2,500 feet, is not important. And, it really is not, except that sometimes their lack of concern persists, with disastrous results, when taking off from short fields.

I once took a course in mountain flying at Colorado Springs. My instructor was a career aviator teaching potential Lufthansa pilots in Arizona. Though he had never flown in Colorado, he had much experience flying in mountainous areas.

We spent a pleasant and interesting day flying through the valleys to various mountain airports, making touch-and-go landings. But as the day wore on and the temperature climbed, we found it more expedient to stop, and taxi back to the end of the runway for takeoff.

My instructor was amiable and patient and very cool-headed. He was obviously enjoying the day. The only evidence he gave of having a nervous system came seconds after takeoff from a short strip under the midafternoon sun. The Apache lifted off but would not climb. I kept the nose down and we droned down the runway, eating up the yardage, maybe five to ten feet off the surface. A hill about a quarter of a mile past the 3,000-foot strip grew in size.

"Don't touch that gear," my companion barked. I had no intention of doing so until we were safely climbing, but the quick and determined response seemed to have been triggered by some unpleasant experience flying in mountainous areas.

A plane accelerates and climbs much better with the gear up. That much everyone knows. But when you are stuck in "bad air," as some mountain pilots call it, it can easily drop you to the surface, which is something that not everyone knows. My instructor did not want to see himself, me, or my plane participate in an unplanned wheels-up landing.

Soon, even with the gear down, we picked up enough speed for a respectable climb. At about fifty feet off the surface I brought up the gear, and we cleared the hill with room to spare.

It is not only on takeoff that high-altitude airports will snag a victim. The approach to landing has its own trap for the uninitiated. The approach should be made at a certain speed. Sooner or later, the pilot gets to feel this speed by reference to the movement of the ground beneath him as he descends toward the touchdown zone. Near the ground, there is a sensation of speed wholly lacking thousands of feet above the ground. He knows his speed on approach just as surely as the automobile driver knows when he is doing 60 mph.

Then one day, at a high-altitude airport, he starts his approach with the airspeed indicating exactly what he wants, 100, 90, 80, or whatever, depending upon the plane. As he descends, he becomes unconsciously aware of the movement of objects beneath his craft. He notices that he is moving faster over the ground than is customary. At Denver he may be moving 8 percent faster. In Leadville, Colorado, almost 10,000 feet high, he will be moving 15 percent faster as a result of altitude alone, to say nothing of even higher density altitude. As is his custom, he will not be watching the airspeed indicator, but will "feel" that he is going too fast.

The wing surface of the plane, which has skin but no eyes, will not feel at all like it is going too fast, nor will the pitot, which would tell the pilot, if he would only look at his airspeed indicator, that he is not going too fast, but just right. So the pilot comes back on the yoke and slows by 8 to 10 miles per hour or more. Now he feels just right. He is moving at the customary speed ever the ground. Not until he levels for landing, or flares, will it feel all wrong, when the plane, in the rarefied air, sinks out from under him and pancakes—onto the runway if he is lucky—onto the brush short of the runway if he is not.

A different type of lapse can cause similar grief at the other end of the runway. Ignorance and inattention take many forms. A pilot may hold his airspeed at precisely the right point and touch down about halfway or two-thirds down the runway. He is simply unconcerned about where on the runway he touches. He is like the playboy with too much money in the bank who pays little attention to how much he spends. Touching down halfway down a 3,000-foot runway is not a great problem if it takes only 700 feet to roll to a stop. But how far the plane rolls depends on how fast it is moving at touchdown (plus other factors that do not change with altitude).

Our playboy pilot may think that he is touching down at the same speed because he kept his airspeed indicator on the same number. But he's wrong. At a high-altitude airport, a pilot may need every bit of the runway, the length of which would cause no problem at sea level. And many a pilot has scratched his head, if he had one left to scratch, over why he went through the fence at the far end of the field.

He learns too late that although the plane flies according to indicated airspeed, once on the ground its brakes allow it to stop in accordance with its *ground* speed, which, in turn, depends not on the *indicated* airspeed but on the true airspeed at which it touched down, the speed at which it was *really* moving.

It is all very confusing, but ought nonetheless to be understood by any pilot who leaves the flatlands and points his nose toward western Colorado, or its like.

In fact, it ought to be understood by every pilot no matter where he flies. He ought to know that a runway is not always as long as it looks, that it expands or contracts with the temperature. Except that unlike all other substances, runways expand in cold weather and contract when it's hot.

Not really, of course, but the effect is the same as if they did.

So, the airspeed indicator is affected by temperature just as the plane is, but the altimeter is not affected by temperature in the way that the plane is. Temperature *does* affect the altimeter, but in a manner that is, in a sense, opposite to the manner in which it affects the airplane. Fortunately, except at extremes of low temperature, the effect is slight and can usually be safely ignored.

The atmosphere, like most other substances, contracts in cold weather and expands in hot weather. The altimeter measures the weight of the total column of air above it. When the atmosphere expands due to heat, the level at which the altimeter might normally have measured 5,000 feet has moved a little higher. In hot weather, if the altimeter says 5,000 feet, the actual altitude of the plane above sea level is somewhat higher.

The result is that in high temperatures the altimeter acts as if it is lower than it actually is, whereas the engine, and consequently the plane, act as though they are higher than they actually are.

If the plane is actually 5,500 feet above sea level on a hot day, the altimeter may read 5,000 feet, whereas the plane and engine perform as though at 8,000 feet. There is no error in the altimeter at ground level due to non-standard temperature, but the error increases with altitude.

Pilots normally make no adjustment in altimeter settings for non-standard temperatures. The amount is usually small—it plays no part in traffic separation, since it affects all planes' altimeters to the same extent. In hot weather, when the plane is slightly higher than the altimeter indicates, there is obviously no danger posed to terrain clearance.

But when it is colder than standard, all this is reversed. The plane is lower than the altimeter says. At 5,000 feet, it performs perhaps, on a very cold day, as well as if it were at only 2,000 feet, which is all to the good, but it will actually *be* somewhat lower than the altimeter says it is. It will not be 3,000 feet lower, but the error could cause a problem in extreme cold if ignored by the pilot. The temperature is capable of going much further from standard in a down direction than in an up direction; in extreme cold, it could make as much as a 1,000-foot difference. Dangerous business when flying over mountainous terrain, especially at night.

Most private pilots will not be flying over mountains in this kind of weather at night, and the temperature rarely creates much of a problem for the altimeter. Altimeter error caused by temperature is usually just another element of confusion to the half-informed. But in rare situations of extreme cold and low visibility, it adds also another element of danger.

Is travel by light plane as safe as driving a car? Or sailing? Or motorboating? Or bicycling? Pick up any of the magazines on any of these subjects that clog the newsstands. How many articles on safety do you see? There are some. But compare them with the high proportion of articles on safety that abound in the magazines for pilots. Magazines dealing with other activities are preoccupied with different means of enjoyment or of obtaining better performance or proper care or maintenance. In magazines devoted to practically no other activity, not even to hunting or to weapons, is one so overwhelmed by warnings of hidden disaster and lurking tragedy, as one is in magazines devoted to flying.

This is not wrong, and shouldn't be otherwise, because flying airplanes is as safe as driving only when the pilot tempers his admiring glances at his plane with thoughts of the treachery of which it is capable. Only when the pilot has learned that his beautiful bird is waiting with bated breath to turn on its master at his first show of carelessness or incompetence should you believe him when he tells you that flying is as safe as driving.

VIII

Gremlins, Glitches and Wild Beasts

ENR

It isn't only the weather and mechanical problems that make life miserable at times for the private pilot. His world sometimes seems beset by a host of enemies conspiring to ruin his best-laid plans. The things that can go wrong with an airplane and its myriad parts would comprise a list whose length has never been plumbed and it is, undoubtedly, still growing.

The internal combustion engine is a remarkable machine. With a minimum of care, it seems to run faultlessly forever. The apprehensive, "What if the engine quits?" of the novice passenger is fully deserving of the contemptuous snicker it elicits from most pilots. It may not be literally true, as many pilots like to say, that "these engines just don't quit." But the confidence is, at least to a large extent, justified. This bit of bravado is probably just a shorthand way of saying what is almost literally true, and that is that a well-maintained engine never quits without plenty of warning—at least as long as you keep gas in the tanks.

"Well maintained" and "plenty of warning" are not totally unrelated phrases. When an engine warns of trouble, you must do something about it, and doing something is part of good maintenance. The warning may show up in the sound, the instruments, the oil consumption, the performance, or in a visual inspection—most often in some combination of these. Backfiring, "detonation," or "pre-ignition," as mechanics call it, or roughness of sound, or an unusual vibration are all early warning symptoms for which a pilot's ear and sense of "feel" soon become attuned.

Sometimes pilots are oblivious and pay no attention to these sounds or vibrations until more serious problems occur. But more often pilots, particularly new pilots, hear sounds and feel vibrations that do not exist, especially at night, or over water, or over long stretches of wasteland.

"Automatic rough," the pilots call it. And many a student flier, or new birdman on his first long hop, especially at night, has heard strange noises that disappear when approaching the airport. More than one pilot has smelled nonexistent smoke under such circumstances, or has noticed that his gauges did not look exactly right, but could not tell exactly why. He usually cannot tell exactly why because there is nothing wrong. Most pilots, even new pilots, continue on their way, though from time to time stories circulate over the coffee cups about those who turned back, or better yet, landed unnecessarily in an open field to avoid an imagined catastrophe.

Imagined catastrophes are unfortunate because there are occasions enough when things *do* go out of kilter, and there is no need to imagine problems that are not there. Most mechanical problems show up early and are benign in their incipient stages. Rarely do they require the cancellation of a flight. Even less frequently do they require a return in midjourney or an unscheduled landing. Usually these early warnings require a trip to the A & P after the flight is completed. (Airframe and Powerplant mechanic, as he is known in the business.)

It sounds simple. You take the plane to the shop to get it fixed and pick it up when it is ready. But nothing with an airplane is so simple. The shop might be many miles away. At many small airports there is no facility for repairs of any consequence; at many larger airports, even in large cities, the facilities may not be very reliable. Most pilots are rather finicky about who works on their planes. Many would rather fly it to an airport in the next town and leave it with their favorite A & P than have the work done at their home base even if someone there claims to be able to do the job. New paint and interiors and the periodic engine overhauls, as well as the warranty work that follows, often require trips of hundreds of miles. It sometimes seems that fully half the light-plane flying is simply to service the plane.

For less serious maintenance, no matter where you take the plane, parts are usually not in stock. As often as not, they must be ordered from the factory and delivery is often agonizingly slow.

There is an endless list of mechanical things that can and do go wrong with planes: there are gas tanks that leak, spark plugs that fail, rings that wear, valves that do not seat, brake drums that wear out, exhaust stacks that crack, mixture controls that need adjustment, fuel pumps and starters that malfunction; and a long catalogue of ills that can beset crankshafts, connecting rods, magnetos, cylinder heads; and a book-length list of other items.

Ownership of an airplane, or even the occasional use of one, is a perpetual search for whatever is wrong and to determine what is going to go wrong next. Every pilot is trained to start every flight with a preflight inspection that is a necessarily perfunctory check of the craft to make sure nothing is visibly and obviously wrong—that the plane has gas and oil, air in the tires, no water in the fuel lines; that the wings are not bent or their surfaces torn; that the movable control surfaces *do* move and in the right direction; and that no lines or wires in the engine are cut or broken. Even pilots like me, who cannot tell the innards of a piston engine from a washing machine, can see if something is disconnected, cut, torn, or broken.

After starting the engine, he should, according to his training, pull almost every lever and switch in the plane, to make sure they work, before takeoff. He checks each set of magnetos. Each engine has two and should run almost as well, at least for a while, on one as on two. If his engine has a carburetor, he checks the carburetor heating system, which prevents ice from forming in the neck of the carburetor at low power settings, which causes engine failure at embarrassing moments. He checks the working of the variable-pitch prop and his vacuum pump, which operates his gyro instruments, and he checks the instruments themselves. He checks his alternators or batteries, which will keep all electrical gadgets working, and the flaps, which may work electrically or hydraulically, and the temperature of the oil and the cylinder heads.

Not every deficiency means a cancellation. As with the

weather, it is a judgment call. Maybe no one aberration of a needle or gauge would cause him to scratch, but a combination of several items might result in the occasional call to ground control of "taxiing back to the ramp." This does not happen often because most of these little problems show up in flight and they are taken care of before the next flight. But it happens just often enough to add another factor of uncertainty in the preparation for many trips by light planes.

More frequently when problems do occur, it is not the engine, but the electronics, which cause everlasting, ever-nagging, insoluble plagues of problems. Unlike well-maintained engines that never quit without warning, well-maintained electronics do. Radios quit or develop static or background noise beyond tolerance. Sometimes they just do odd and unpredictable things, and they straighten out when, or before, they get to the repair facility. It may be moisture; it may be a speck of dirt; or it may be, as was thought in World War II, the work of gremlins. Whether it is gremlins, moisture, dirt, or poor workmanship, unreliability is 95 percent of the reason why practically all light planes these days, other than those used for primary training, aerobatics, or crop dusting, have two navcoms.

At any time, one of the two "coms," the talking parts of the radios, could go out. So might one of the navs. Is it all right to take off with only one nav or only one com working?

It depends on the pilot. And, in the opinion of most pilots, it depends largely on the weather. In good weather, losing all communications or electronic navigation, or both, is not a tragedy. In messy weather, when you cannot see the ground or, sometimes, other planes nearby, it could be.

But total failure is not the only problem. The navigation part of the radio, the omnis, can get out of kilter from time to time by a few degrees, just enough to make it unreliable for an instrument flight. And both the nav and the com can have a crystal or two go sour, which means that a few frequencies cannot be received. This will be discovered, as a rule, only in flight, when you try to get those frequencies.

And there is a lot more to worry about than radios, even in

the electronics department. Even the simplest light planes today have another little black box called a transponder. The purpose of this gadget is to answer the ground radar that keeps track of you almost wherever you fly in this country on instruments and particularly in the vicinity of busy terminals. It identifies your plane to the radar controller. It is illegal to fly through certain terminal-control areas, at the nation's biggest cities, without it.

There is in many light planes distance-measuring equipment, DME, which tells your distance from the VHF stations sending navigation signals. This is considered a luxury by some. But a poor man's luxury is a rich man's necessity, and depending on circumstances and the condition of other equipment, it could be a vital factor on a particular flight.

The same is true for the ADF, the automatic direction finder, that low-frequency receiver that points like a bird dog to the radio beacon or commercial broadcast station to which you tune. It is not a necessity unless you are going to an airport in instrument conditions where the only instrument approach is the "NDB Approach"—one involving a low frequency non-directional beacon picked up by the ADF. There are a lot of these approaches at small airports around the country. In some parts of the world, it is the primary, and in some cases, the only, method of radio navigation.

There is often an automatic pilot, which can keep a plane level and headed in the right direction while a pilot looks at his chart or copies clearances. There is a three-light marker beacon, a piece of equipment with bright lights that flash and a noisemaker that beeps on certain instrument approaches, telling the pilot of his location at crucial points on the final approach.

There are the flight instruments. The air speed indicator, the altimeter, and the rate-of-climb indicator all work off a pitot-static air system that is relatively free of problems. Except for ice or impurities clogging the static, or moving-air intake, there is little than can happen. If it does, there is usually an alternate source of static air that will operate the instruments with some predictable error in reading.

The other major group of instruments is the gyro instruments: the artificial horizon (AH), the gyro compass or directional gyro (DG), and the turn indicator. These are the ones you count on to keep you right side up in that nether world of instruments. On most modern light planes, the gyros that operate them are powered by an engine-driven suction pump. The gyro is a more complicated system than that operating the flight instruments, and gyro instruments can and do go sour. And on occasion the suction pump itself goes out and you lose them all.

For this reason, the gyro that controls the turn indicator, a needle that points right or left as the nose of the plane moves right or left across the horizon, is, in many planes, electrically operated. In the event of a failure of the suction pump while in clouds at least the turn indicator remains a lifeline to the outside world. It is something to tell the pilot if he is going straight or turning. If all three instruments were part of the same system, it might be too many eggs in one basket.

Loss of the gyro instruments under actual instrument conditions can be a considerable problem. The artificial horizon and the gyro compass are not only two major ties to reality under instrument conditions, but are major crutches for the pilot in murky or clouded skies, even when the ground is visible. Unlike in days past, today's student pilots quickly learn, sometimes to their detriment, that it is easier to keep wings and nose precisely level by looking at the artificial horizon than by looking at the real one, which may be very hazy. They learn that it is easier to fly a straight line by holding a constant heading on the gyro compass than by flying to a dimly defined point in the distance. Consciously or otherwise, most students find themselves spending more time looking at those two instruments than the outside world.

And when they start flying under the hood, many of them have little trouble these days, so used have they become to flying these instruments and ignoring the outside. They have little trouble, that is, until they are required to do a type of instrument flying known as "partial panel."

Partial panel means that not only is the real horizon taken away, but also the artificial one, along with the directional gyro.

This is an exercise that simulates loss of the suction pump in clouds. Precise flying under these conditions, to new pilots and even many experienced ones, is more difficult. They are used to looking at the artificial horizon and gyro compass in flight because it is easy to do so.

The artificial horizon is the nearest thing a pilot has to a picture of himself in space. The horizontal line across the face of this circular instrument stays level just like the real horizon. The other part of the instrument, a little pair of wings, rolls with the airplane, and rise above and falls below the line representing the horizon, just as the nose of the real plane rises and falls below the real horizon.

It is also easy because at one glance you can see your position relative to the real world, or a reasonable facsimile of it. You can see in two dimensions and the directional gyro supplies a reasonably accurate reference to the third. One glance at the AH, and you can tell whether your nose is low, high, or just right, and whether your wings tilt right, left, or not at all. One glance at the DG and you can tell whether you are turning. The faster the plane turns, the faster the gyro compass turns. Keep the same number at the top of the dial of the DG and you are not turning. Turn right to increase the numbers, turn left to decrease them.

But take away these two gyro-driven instruments and it's a brand-new business, a brand-new world. They are "taken away" by means of a round black piece of rubber with black suction cups on one side to make it stick to the face of the instrument. Nothing tells you now about your lateral attitude but the turn indicator. At the bottom of this instrument is a little black ball suspended in liquid that tells you whether the turn is coordinated or whether you're slipping or skidding or banked too much, or too little, for the rate of turn. You also have the pressure instruments: airspeed indicator, altimeter, and rate of climb.

That is how you fly on a partial panel: needle, ball, airspeed, and altimeter. That is the order of your scan.

There are many private pilots today who do a creditable job

of flying instruments—when they *have* all their instruments, and they're in working order. There are not as many who do as well on partial panel. There are many pilots who regularly practice under the hood, but not as many who practice under the hood with black suction cups on the artificial horizon and the gyro compass.

For visual flight, the AH and DG are not necessary. But they, as well as a number of others, are required for instrument flight by federal air regulations. Thinking about it one Sunday afternoon as I sat with my son Neil and a friend in the Astrodome in Houston, I could not remember whether these two instruments were included or not in that list of minimum requirements for instrument flight. We had flown from New Orleans for the afternoon baseball game, and I suppose that as far as my two passengers were concerned, the trip was routine.

It was murky, and forward visibility was low, but the ground was visible and both of my passengers had flown with me through much worse weather. Until that flight, I had no idea how much, even without intending to, pilots come to rely on instruments, the artificial horizon in particular.

About halfway to Houston, I had noticed the horizon line of the AH to be slightly lower than the permanently mounted wings of the instrument. Instinctively I looked at the airspeed, which was no lower than it should have been for level flight, definitely too high to be climbing, as the AH indicated. The hands of the altimeter were stationary at my cruising altitude of 6,000 feet. The rate of climb was at zero. I manually adjusted the wings to bring them down to the horizon line where I, and most pilots, usually put them to indicate level flight. It is usually adjusted once, at the beginning of a flight, and rarely touched again.

A few minutes later, the horizon was again slightly low and I could manipulate the controls to make it show level flight only by causing the altimeter and rate of climb indicator to show a descent and the airspeed to increase. Three instruments could not be wrong. I raised the nose until the other instruments indicated level flight. The AH was obviously out of whack.

The AH out of whack? That was like saying the world was

out of whack. The AH is the instrument you use to make all the other needles and dials fall into place. I looked again. Maybe I was wrong. Now the AH showed a sharp nose-up attitude, which at the power setting I had, would have meant about a 1,000-foot-per-minute climb, but the other three instruments agreed with each other that I was in level flight.

The other three instruments are gauges. The AH is like a picture. I, like most others, am more prone to believe pictures than gauges. Fortunately, there was just enough outside visibility to confirm that the three quiet little gauges were accurate and the artificial horizon was shouting a lie. I would have known it anyway. The logic of it was overwhelming. You do not disregard three instruments because of one. I just did not realize how emotionally dependent I had become on that pictorial representation of myself in relation to the world around me.

I did not realize it until I heard the alarm in the voice of my son breaking through my concentration on the instruments. "Dad, why are you sweating?" he demanded. Why was I? I did not even know I was. His question brought home the foolishness of the whole situation. I had a perfectly good directional gyro, turn indicator, rate-of-climb indicator, airspeed indicator, altimeter, and two good radios with operating navigational aids. Even in solid instrument weather, I could have completed the trip without incident using only half of those instruments. To make the whole situation more ludicrous, it was not really instrument weather at all. I could have flown quite well just by looking outside with only an occasional reference to the altimeter and the omnis.

But this early in my flying career, I was already used to staring at instruments. I was not used to looking outside. My instrument rating was relatively new at the time, and as part of the training there was considerable partial-panel work. Maybe that was the problem. Maybe it had been drilled into me that loss of the AH—or any of the numerous other instruments—was in a category known as "emergency."

It obviously wasn't an emergency, and it was silly even to think about it so much. We make too much of these gadgets. I used to fly planes that didn't even have artificial horizons and in weather that was not much better than this. I relaxed and decided not to think about it.

Except that every time I looked at the gadget—it was hard not to—and saw that horizon line down near the bottom of the disk where I was not used to seeing it, I had the craziest sensation that I was climbing almost straight up. Hanging on the props, they call it. The urge to push the controls forward was, at least momentarily, quite strong. That is, until I looked again at the reassuring calm of the other instruments or looked straight down at the ground.

Finally, the horizon line disappeared beneath the lower edge of the face of the instrument. Good! Now it could not distract me anymore. The little wings of the permanently affixed airplane sat all alone in the middle of the blank instrument as though they had finally escaped this world and were alone in space—free at last of any horizon.

Free, that is, until about twenty minutes or so later, that little thin line of a horizon appeared again—this time at about a 45-degree slant in the upper-left portion of the face of the instrument. Now I had the craziest feeling that I was doing steep turns upside down and that the horizon was over my right shoulder. Why didn't it stay out of sight and let me alone? Gradually, it descended, still at a 45-degree angle, passed over the miniature airplane, through the lower portion of the instrument, and again disappeared. It was eerie. I wondered where and how it would show up next.

Happily, it never did. I was now approaching Houston and was being vectored for an instrument approach. Something seemed to tell me that some regulation I had read somewhere or other required that an equipment failure must be reported to air-traffic control, so I told Houston approach control. They were totally unconcerned.

I made the approach and landed at Hobby Airport. It was Sunday and no instrument shop was open there. Sitting in the Astrodome, while my two passengers were absorbed in the ball game, I thought of nothing but my screwy artificial horizon that appeared like a galloping ghost in unexpected places at unexpected times, and the fact that I would be flying back at night. I tried to remember whether the AH was one of those instruments required for instrument flight and whether the weather would be good enough to go VFR if it were necessary.

When the game ended—and I neither remember nor ever cared who won—I called flight service. The weather sounded good, just scattered buildups. But the weather wasn't good enough for me to fly VFR at night. I do not do that, except on cloudless nights. You cannot always see the clouds to avoid them. According to flight service, the usual towering cumulus of a summer afternoon were expected to last into evening, but not to exceed 8,000 or 9,000 feet in altitude.

I managed to take off before dark. Night came quickly, and the weather was not what it was cracked up to be. The so-called scattered buildups were more numerous, and a good number of them hovered high above 9,000 feet and bounced us around, without the slightest consideration for the fact that I had no artificial horizon.

If on the flight up I learned how much I had relied on the AH, on the flight back I learned how reliable and accurate an instrument the directional gyro is and how useful an addition it is to the needle-ball and airspeed of the basic flight instruments. Losing the AH is tough, but losing the whole gyro system would obviously be much tougher; and I was grateful that I had lost only one instrument and not the pump or the system. Our AH just needed an overhaul, which it got in New Orleans.

I later had an opportunity to compare the lack of artificial horizon and operating directional gyro, with an operating artificial horizon and no directional gyro.

On a return trip from Destin, Florida, the DG went gradually loco and I had the mindless tendency to keep the desired heading at the top of the dial, even though that was meaningless and to do so would at times have steered me on my way to Mexico's Yucatán Peninsula, and other times would have headed me back where I came from. In good weather, it was easy to follow the coastline when I forced myself to ignore the erratic gyro compass. Had the weather been bad, it would have been less easy, though quite possible, to follow the free-floating magnetic compass.

I had returned to flying less than a year before, and had a total accumulated flying time of less than 200 hours, when the flimsiness of the whole setup grabbed my attention as I flew a Skylane, one hazy and rainy afternoon. A Skylane is a very stable 230 hp single-engine high-wing Cessna with four seats. This one belonged to an experienced pilot and friend of mine, Max, and we were flying to Memphis to peruse the stock of a second-hand plane dealer. Max and I had talked from time to time about buying a plane together.

Max was a semi-professional, and claimed to have almost 8,000 flying hours. On this particular afternoon, he had drops in his eyes and could not see a thing outside of the plane, though he could make out the instruments well enough. It was not supposed to have mattered because I was to fly the plane. That I had less than 200 hours' flying time did not bother Max, so I decided it needn't bother me. In the back seat was a neighbor of Max's who had never been in a light plane. He said he had always wanted to do so and he had come along for the ride.

Less than a half hour out of New Orleans, I noticed that I was doing an unusually good job of staying on course by keeping the omni needles centered. Then it occurred to me that nobody could be that accurate, and that the needles must be centered only because they are always centered when the instrument is off. Only then did I notice the red flag, in the little window on the face of the instrument, that reads "off."

I had no instrument rating at the time, and the weather was not the best. The ceiling was low and ragged. Visibility was low because of the smoke, the haze, and a light drizzle. I picked up the mike to call flight service, to check what weather was being forecast and to advise of our predicament and my intentions to land. A few calls on the mike and I realized the communications were also out—so were the battery-operated engine instruments—and a check of the various warning lights brought no response. We obviously had a complete electrical failure.

The passenger in the back seat expressed the opinion that we should "get this thing on the ground" as soon as possible. He instilled us with pride in ourselves by noting that he observed the battery needle indicating a discharge on takeoff; that it seemed funny to him, but that he did not say anything because he "figured you guys knew what you were doing."

Without electronic navigation, I like big, easy-to-see, continuous landmarks, like the Mississippi River, which I knew was to the west. It was to the west that I headed. I assumed we were near Natchez, which is on the river, and I meant to land there or at whatever airport came up next. Max's lack of concern about the whole affair made me wonder whether this type of thing was routine to him—and his airplane.

After turning north along the river, I soon spotted a single-runway airport. I knew it wasn't Natchez—the Natchez Airport had four runways—but it didn't matter. One runway was enough. As we paralleled the single runway at the customary 800-foot pattern altitude, I looked for the windsock. I couldn't find it. Neither could Max—I figured his eyedrops were responsible. Nor could his smart friend in the back seat. I saw no nearby smokestacks or any other clearly visible indication of wind direction, but something made me think the wind was from the south.

I turned left toward the north end of the runway and then left again to line up with it and land toward the south. I kept the airspeed at 80 mph, the best approach speed in a Skylane with flaps down. It was the fastest 80 mph I ever flew. I slowed to 70, and even that looked too fast. I flared about one-third of the way down the runway, which I judged to be about 3,000 feet long. I used up another one-third of it before the plane finally started to settle. We had eaten up well over two-thirds of the runway before it touched solidly and we felt like we were still doing 60. We may well have been.

Max and I both stood up on the brakes and slowed it just barely enough to permit a safe turn-off at the end of the runway. Had we run off the end and smashed the plane, or ourselves, the FAA would have cited "improper approach," namely, landing downwind, and "failing to initiate a go-around," which I should have done as soon as I realized the problem.

As we taxied to the ramp, we discovered we were in Vicksburg. We also found the windsock, which was of white canvas on top of a white-roofed hangar. Max was indignant at the "stupidity" of the white on white. The passenger muttered only that he *thought* we were coming in mighty fast.

There were no electronic repair facilities at Vicksburg. Max suggested a hop of about fifty miles due west to Hawkins Field, at Jackson, where we could most likely get the electricity working and then return to New Orleans. We forgot about completing the trip to Memphis. Our rear-seat passenger said he had a brother living in Vicksburg, and since we were there, he thought he would stay and visit. He never did thank us for the ride.

Max phoned the Jackson Airport tower and advised the controller that we were coming in without a radio. The controller said he would give us a light signal. He didn't. We landed anyway. When we telephoned the tower after landing the controller informed us that nobody had called, but not to worry. We were the third plane to come in that day without radio—an indictment, I suppose, of the aviation electronics business, aircraft owners, or both.

The people at the Jackson repair facility worked on the electrical system for about an hour, announced that they couldn't get it to work, put it back in the plane, and suggested that we go to Jackson Municipal Airport, on the other side of town. We telephoned the tower controller at Hawkins, told him we were taking off without radio, asked for a light signal, and requested that he notify the Municipal tower that we would be landing without radio. The Hawkins tower controller informed us that he would indeed call Municipal and tell them that we were *finally* arriving. He explained that the Municipal tower had called Hawkins shortly after we arrived to see if we landed. Municipal had been expecting us and we did not show. Max had obviously called the wrong airport from Vicksburg.

We climbed aboard and started the engine. I turned on the radio. It worked. The people who thought they didn't fix the electrical system must have accidently bumped the right wire. It was not the first time something on a plane got fixed by accident. We told an amused tower controller at Hawkins to cancel with Municipal, that we were flying back to New Orleans before the radio quit again.

The trip was not over. About thirty miles south of McComb, Mississippi, we received a call from the flight-service station. Present weather in New Orleans was a 500-foot overcast with a one-half-mile visibility and a severe thunderstorm in progress. I was in the process of doing a 180-degree turn when I noticed Max looking at me as though I had suddenly said something in Greek, and I heard him ask me where I was going. I told him I was going back to McComb to land, that I understood that he couldn't see, and asked if the drops in his eyes affected his hearing also. Max was incredulous. "You've got 500 feet," he told me. I listened as Max explained how I could come in low over Lake Pontchartrain beneath the thunderstorm to the airport, and as I listened, I headed for McComb and landed.

Over hamburgers, I explained to Max that it was getting dark, that I had little experience in night flying, and that I didn't trust his unpredictable electrical system. The idea of coming in at night without radio or lights appealed to me not at all, even in good weather, and we had no idea when or if good weather would arrive that night. I suggested we take the bus. We did, arriving home about midnight.

The next day, Max had a friend fly him back to pick up his plane. The electricity had quit again and Max came back to New Orleans without radio.

About a year later, Max rented a Cessna 150, a 100 hp two-seater trainer. He said he was going to Picayune, Mississippi, about eighty miles northeast of New Orleans. He was never heard from again. A search of large areas and a check of all airports in that part of the country produced nothing. In the years since then, a number of planes and pilots have disappeared, but always, they, or the bodies and the wreckage, have been found—sooner or later. Max and his 300-mile-range trainer were never seen again.

Usually, it is not the entire electrical system that goes. Usually, it is just one or two instruments—one radio, the distance-measuring equipment, the automatic direction finder, the transponder, or something. Nothing tragic, just annoying. One just doesn't realize how many gadgets and parts there are on a plane until they malfunction or quit. But engines seem to keep on going. One couldn't truthfully say that they never quit. Sometimes they do. That possibility came home to me one day when the engine-driven fuel pump on the right engine of my twin-engine Beech Baron failed, high over the mountains of central Mexico. I was always told by the graybeards at the airport that if an engine ever failed, it would be at night or over water, or over mountains with a full load. This pump chose to quit, at 12,000 feet, about 100 miles north of Mexico City. I had four passengers and all five of us had baggage for a three-day Easter weekend in Mexico City.

Below were 8,000-foot ridges, and ahead were two 10,000-foot peaks just north of the city. A sudden lurch to the right brought my attention forcefully to the engine instruments. The right-engine fuel pressure was zero and the exhaust gas temperature gauge was at the bottom. It didn't take long to establish the failure of the engine-driven fuel pump as the cause, since the engine ran beautifully when I switched on the electric boost pump, normally used only for starting. This boost pump is usually on only for a few seconds. It was not intended to operate for long periods during flight. How long was it good for? Five minutes? Thirty minutes? Two hours? The aircraft manual said to avoid "extended operation" of the electric pump and to use it "no longer than necessary." Big help.

Do I go ahead to Mexico City? Or do I turn back to Tampico, on the Gulf? I was halfway between the two cities. I had four passengers who were looking forward to an Easter weekend in Mexico City, not Tampico. Mexico City International Airport had excellent repair facilities, including a Beechcraft dealer. Tampico probably had nothing.

These are all trivial considerations if a catastrophe is in the offing, and the 100 miles ahead of me was over rising and increasingly rugged terrain. Back toward Tampico, the mountain ridges fell gradually away to flat plains and sea level. But somehow the situation didn't seem urgent, and while I mulled it over, we grew closer and closer to Mexico, making the decision easier and easier and, finally, moot.

Repair facilities at Mexico City were excellent but expensive. Nobody works in Mexico over Easter, and from Holy Thursday until the following Monday, I could not be sure that the Mexico Beechcraft facility had a pump in stock. Fortunately it did. By the time it was installed, it was late afternoon and we flew back to New Orleans at night.

Why did I continue on over mountainous terrain? Why wasn't safety my one and only concern? Why were frivolous considerations of a pleasant holiday and convenient repair facilities allowed to enter into the picture at all? I have made a few in-flight decisions that in retrospect seemed foolish. This was not one of them. I would probably do it again. I am not sure why. A number of factors gave me confidence, one of which, perhaps the least important, was the total lack of any tone of urgency in the very conservative aircraft manual, vague though it was, in its treatment of flight on the electric boost pump.

Another consideration, and definitely not the least, was the second engine on this twin-engine Baron. Would I have continued the flight under these circumstances if the same misfortune befell my only engine in a single-engine craft? I do not know, but the chances of my having opted for a course reversal and landing at Tampico would have been much greater.

Which raises the whole issue so often debated in flying magazines and over greasy hotcakes at airport restaurants: two engines or one? In the entire realm of flight safety, it is one of the most controversial and frequently discussed topics, and one over which many thoughtful pilots have agonized.

There are those will fly in light planes only if they are equipped with two engines. Among nonpilots, the number is enormous. Their reasoning is very simple: if one engine quits on a twin-engine plane, you can keep flying on the other. If the engine quits on a single-engine plane, you crash.

But life in general, and aeronautics, in particular, is never so simple. There are, to be sure, experienced pilots who feel more comfortable with twins. There are those who will make certain trips only in twins—extended night flights or over-water flights being the most ususal. There are some few pilots who will not make any extended flight in a single-engine plane, but they are rare and getting rarer.

The preferences of the pilots who like two engines rest on much more solid underpinnings than the prejudices of the passengers. If the passengers who would fly only in a twin understood all the ramifications of the single versus twin controversy, they would probably not broaden their area of tolerance to include single-engine planes. They probably would never fly light planes at all. Pilots frequently like to tell their nonflying friends that a single is just as safe, or safer, than a twin. What they really mean is that a twin in many situations is just as dangerous, or more dangerous, than a single.

It is true that a twin-engine plane can fly on one engine—under certain conditions. But even when those conditions exist, a twin is a far different machine with only one prop turning than it is with two.

It flies, but just barely. The service ceiling of most light twins, those without expensive turbochargers, is about 18,000 to 20,000 feet with two engines. With one engine out, their service ceiling is usually between 5,000 and 7,500 feet.

Well, you say, at least you're flying. Maybe you are and maybe you aren't. It depends on how high the terrain is and how high the airplane thinks it is—it is back to that. As we have seen, and as many pilots have found, to their grief, a plane flies according to how high it "feels" it is, not how high it actually *is* above sea level. That depends to a large degree on the temperature.

It takes no particular talent to realize that a plane with a 6,000-foot single-engine ceiling is not going to fly very high on one engine at Pitken County Airport in Aspen, Colorado, which is 7,800 feet above sea level. The pilot of such a plane who thinks he has 1,000 feet to play with on a hot summer's day in Denver or Pueblo, both at 5,000 feet, if one engine goes, lives in a fool's paradise. He has nothing at all, because the plane feels like it is much higher than 6,000 feet.

It is not only the ceiling that suffers. Performance suffers grievously in every respect with an engine out, the rate of climb in particular. A twin with one engine gone does not lose one-half its climb performance, it loses 80 percent of it. A twin with a 1,6000-foot-per-minute climb at sea level may climb at only 300 feet per minute with one engine out. A twin with a 1,400-foot-per-minute climb may only be able to rise with one engine out a little more than 200 feet per minute.

So what, you say. At least it is better than no climb capacity at all, which is what you get when the only engine on a single quits working. Sometimes it is, sometimes it isn't. At takeoff, with a 1,600-foot-per-minute climb, there is performance to spare, plenty of money in the bank, so to speak. At 250 feet per minute, every moment and every action of the pilot is crucial. If the engine goes during the first five or ten seconds after take-off, it is often a close guess as to whether you have a couple of dimes to see you through, or whether you are flat broke. That 250-to-300-foot-per-minute climb is a maximum figure, and one you only get with the gear up and the dead prop feathered (with blades parallel to the line of flight). If the dead prop is not feathered, it is windmilling—the flat edge of the blade is exposed to the wind and the drag caused by the wind's pushing against it erodes what little climb performance there is. Without the gear up, there isn't any climb performance at all. Most light twins in most situations just won't climb with the gear hanging down and one engine out—feathered or unfeathered.

Consequently the pilot has some quick hand motions to make if an engine goes at takeoff. He has to be fast and alert. It has happened that an engine has quit at a crucial point, and the pilot feathered the wrong engine, namely, the good one. Then he had none. In the relatively short history of flying, this has happened to amateurs and airline pilots alike.

But, you say, if he is quick and alert, gets the gear up, and feathers the correct prop, at least the plane will climb. Then, you say, you are better off with your one engine.

You may be, but if your pilot doesn't know the capability, and more importantly, the limitations, of his plane, you may be worse off—much worse.

A twin-engine plane with one engine out is like a wounded

beast; it not only cannot do much good, but unless handled very gently and very skillfully, it can turn on you, and quite viciously. A twin with one engine out goes crazy. Therein lies most of the single- versus multi-engine controversy.

The twin goes crazy because when one engine goes out, the other one wants to pull you around the plane's center line toward the bad engine. The power on the good engine makes the nose yaw toward the bad engine, which in turn makes the wing with the power still working want to rise. The pilot keeps the plane straight and level only by holding hard rudder and aileron on the side of the good engine. The higher the power setting on the good engine, the greater the tendency to yaw and roll; with an engine out, especially if you are trying to climb, you want all the power you can get.

As every pilot knows from his earliest flying days, the slower a plane flies, the less effective the control surfaces are. The faster the flow of air over the surfaces, the more effective they are. With one engine gone, the slower the speed, the more flexion of the controls necessary to keep the plane from rolling. Finally, you get down to a speed at which with full power on one engine, you cannot stop the yaw or the roll even with full flexion of the aileron and the rudder pedal to the floor. Below that critical speed, things happen fast. The plane flips over on its back. There are usually no survivors. That speed is known as the Vmc, or the minimum control speed. It is well named.

It may seem like a simple thing to keep your speed in a twin above Vmc, which is usually between 80 to 92 miles per hour, depending on the plane's make and model. All the books warn: Do not take off until the speed is above Vmc; do not let the speed get below Vmc on approach; if the engine fails en route, do not let your speed get below Vmc trying to hold altitude.

This is all very well, but what do you do when the engine quits right after liftoff, and ahead of you is rising terrain, or other obstacles? You get your gear up and feather the prop, of course. Now you can climb, maybe 250 feet per minute if the airport is at sea level and the temperature is a standard 59°. If it is hot, or if the airport is several thousand feet above sea level you climb more slowly. In one minute, at your best-rate-of-climb speed, you will travel about two miles. There is a best *angle* of climb speed, which is a few miles less and which helps a little, but very little. In round figures, you had better hope that nothing rises more than 200 to 300 feet within two miles of the airport.

It is different with heavy transports. They must demonstrate a minimum climb capability with an engine out in order to be certified for service. This is not so for the twin-engine light planes, which don't have to demonstrate anything. Federal regulations require only that the manufacturer state what the climb is on one engine, but do not require that there be any at all.

When the engine quits on takeoff, it is necessarily a shock to the Sunday pilot. I doubt that any amount of training can remove the element of shock. The adrenaline is pumping. You don't know exactly how far away the obstacles are or exactly how high. You eyeball them. With the adrenaline pumping, you eyeball them. Under these circumstances, they will undoubtedly look higher and closer than they really are. The instinctive urge to come back on the controls to climb must be overpowering.

If you keep your head, there is no possibility of getting below Vmc because you will not even want to go below your single engine's best rate, or best-angle-of-climb speed, which may be ten to fifteen miles per hour higher than Vmc. If you keep your head, you know that once the plane gets below best-angle-of-climb speed, you are working against yourself. The more you come back on the controls, the slower you go, the less your rate of climb, or in some circumstances, the faster your sink.

You keep your speed up, and if you see you cannot clear the water tower, or the buildings, or the hill, you chop the throttle on the good engine, land wherever you are, and take the consequences. Unless you panic, you do not try to clear the hurdles by pulling back on the controls while oblivious to airspeed. Unless you panic, in other words, you do not allow the plane to flip over on its back.

Ah, yes—unless you panic, unless you lose your head. All the magazine articles advise you not to do that. How often is the pilot able to follow this sound advice when the engine quits too late to land again on the runway, and too soon after liftoff to clear the hurdles? It must be terribly tempting to come back on the controls rather than landing in the nearest field or ditch.

When the engine on a single quits, all is silence. The pilot no longer has an airplane, he is flying a glider. The greatest optimist knows he has no power and that he is going to land—like it or not. The only question is where.

When a twin goes crazy after takeoff, however, the pilot knows he is still flying. He can feel it, touch it and hear it. How many can resist the temptation to keep flying?

According to statistics, a lot of pilots cannot. Engine failure just before or shortly after the takeoff is an extremely dangerous matter. If the takeoff is over flat, open fields, or over water, it is a lot less dangerous but excepting these rare situations, it is practically always better to chop the power and take your chances. Pull back on the controls, get below Vmc, go over on your back, and you have no chance.

But this is only for a few seconds at most, say the multi-engine enthusiasts. Except for those few seconds, you are much better off with that second engine. That is largely true, but experience has shown that if an engine is going to fail, it is most likely to do so on takeoff, when it is running wide open and screaming at full power, or at the first reduction of power after takeoff. Most pilots delay reducing power until they have at least 400 feet of altitude—some opt for a thousand feet—for that very reason, but most engine failures are still at takeoff.

The illusory nature of the safety of that second engine is not limited to the takeoff situation. The approach has its own special problems. It is made with gear down, and a careless use of power or a disregard of airspeed can leave you at the mercy of the whims of your engine, though the perils are not so bad as those of the takeoff.

There are other marginal areas. The man flying high, wide and handsome over the 14,000-foot peaks of the Rockies, or the Sierra Nevadas, or the 8,000- to 10,000-foot ridges of Wyoming, Montana, or Mexico, may seem mighty secure behind those two engines; but his chances of getting into trouble may be exactly twice as great as those of his friends flying the single. In case one goes, he will fly on one engine all right, but not high enough to clear the ridges, and unless he is disciplined enough to accept a forced landing on a reasonably level area where available, he may fly right into a ridge on his one good engine.

The man who flies above high ridges and peaks obscured by clouds in a twin-engine plane may be twice as foolhardy as the man who flies a single over a very low ceiling over any kind of terrain. The latter bets his life on his one engine; the former may be betting his life on both of them individually.

I flew a twin for a number of years and made a few trips into the mountains. I swore that I would never put myself in a situation where I needed both engines to fly safely. Yet one day I took off from Pueblo, Colorado, through an overcast, climbed above it, and headed for the mountains. I was armed with a weather briefing assuring me that conditions were clear beyond the first range of mountains, as is very often the case. The moist air backs up against the first mountain range and it is usually clear beyond.

Only this time it wasn't. Through breaks in the clouds, I could see only a few of the 10,000-foot peaks below me. Only the 14,000-foot giants of the Great Divide showed their crests above the broken stratus. So, despite all my promises to myself, there I was. Failure of either engine would have meant a descent through clouds, and whether it would be a safe journey through, or a collision with a cloud-enshrouded peak, would be a matter of pure luck. I was staking my life, and that of my passenger, at least for a short time, on both engines' working. My odds would have been better with one.

Is there nothing to be said by the boys on the other side of the table? Is the apparent safety of that second engine entirely an illusion?

Despite it all, a twin-engine plane flown by a pilot proficient in flying it on one engine and knowledgeable of its limitations has a measure of safety the single engine cannot match. The fallacy of twin-engine safety is not as much in the performance of the plane on one engine as it is in the relative competence represented by the multi-engine rating of many multi-engine pilots.

It is a pitiful weakness in the currency requirement of the federal air regulations that a pilot need not practice single-engine procedures at all to maintain his twin-engine rating. To get the rating in the first place, he must be instructed in all phases of single-engine operation. Then he can fly a twin the rest of his life and never again practice flying it on one engine.

To fly instruments, for instance, a pilot must not only have a rating but must have six hours of simulated or actual instrument time, including six approaches for landing, logged in the previous six months. To fly at night, he must have three takeoffs and landings at night in the last ninety days. To carry passengers at all in any plane, he must have three takeoffs and landings in the last ninety days in that make and model.

There is total oblivion in the Federal Air Regulations to the fact that a multi-engine plane is not the same plane with one engine working as it is with two. To fly passengers in a twin-engine plane, the pilot need only have his three takeoffs and landings in the last ninety days in that type plane. Not the slightest experience in single-engine work in his twin need he have since the day he obtained his rating.

With the pilot who is proficient and aware, there is much to be said for the twin. I know that the engines are reliable. I also know that the hallowed phrase that they "just don't quit" really means, more precisely, that in round numbers, there is one engine failure in every 50,000 hours of operation. In any one hour of operation, I suppose the odds are 50,000 to one that the engine will keep going. In a two-hour trip, the odds are down to 25,000 to one. They sound high. Is it high enough to stake your life on it? Maybe the odds are a lot better if you are careful. Maybe it is the fools, all those other guys, who do not maintain their engines, who cause the statistics. No matter what the odds against it, I do not like to be painted into a corner. If the unlikely happens, I still want one more chance, and, preferably, one more beyond that.

In most cases of engine failure in a single-engine plane you have that one more chance. Over decent terrain in daylight, with a reasonably high ceiling and visibility, you are not by any means doomed by the failure of the engine. A light plane does not need a mile of paved runway to land. An open field, a highway, or a good-sized parking lot sometimes suffices. It is risky, but a combination of skill and luck more often than not has saved the hide of the pilot and his passengers under these circumstances. Most light planes have a glide ratio of about ten to one, ten feet of glide without power for every foot of altitude. At 5,000 feet, there is a radius of about ten miles in which to look for something. Even treetop landings have been survived, in some cases without injury.

At night, or over a cloud deck with very low bottoms, things are different, all luck. When you cannot see what you are gliding into, you take what comes. An open field a little to the right of a brick wall does you no good if you cannot see it. Over open water, or jagged peaks, even relatively low ones, you may be almost literally staking your life on your one engine. The odds are way down now. These are the circumstances: night, low clouds, water and mountains—when that second engine may mean the difference between a harrowing flight to the nearest airport on one engine or leaving your fate to dumb luck. That latter situation is Russian roulette with most of the chambers loaded. Even in the best of circumstances, flying twenty-five or fifty miles on one engine to the nearest airport is better than an off-airport landing.

Did we say mountains? Is the second engine any good over mountains? To our mythical, proficient pilot who knows his plane, it is. The ceiling of the plane goes up as the weight goes down, and our pilot will stay light in the mountains. If worse comes to worse, it is better to descend on one engine at 50 to 100 feet per minute, than to have to come down at 500 feet per minute with no power at all. That one engine may not keep you at altitude, but it will stretch the glide tremendously and give many more options to the pilot who is cool enough to weigh them.

In a lifetime of flying, the overwhelming majority of pilots will never have an engine failure, nor will the overwhelming majority of insured homeowners ever experience a fire. Like the insurance policy, the second engine is peace of mind. But the premium comes very high. Maintenance on one engine is high enough. Maintenance on two is twice as high. Fuel consumption is not quite twice as high, since twins go a little faster than their equivalent single-engine machines, but not much.

For almost twice as much expense, you get very little extra performance. A plane with two 260 hp engines may cost 70 percent more than one with a single 260 hp engine. It will probably go only about 10 percent faster, carry 10 percent more weight, have maybe seven percent or eight percent more range, and will fly no higher at all, even with both engines. All you get for your money, aside from that little extra performance, is safety—better odds, but no guarantees.

Is it worth it? There has been more ink spilled and more breath blown over that subject than over almost any other involving light-plane safety. There is no sign of a general consensus. The controlling factor in most cases is the pocketbook. Two-engine planes are expensive, yet there are some to whom money is not an object but who nonetheless consider a light twin a waste of money and fuel.

Personally, I like the twin. With a friend, I owned a twin-engine Beech Baron for over four years, and a twin-engine Piper Apache for a year and a half before that. The little extra performance was nice, but nicer was that little extra assurance. For over four years, I did my share of flying at night, over low cloud decks, mountains, and water. With the exception of a hop of over 600 miles across the waters of the Gulf of Mexico, I probably would have made every one of them in a single. I still do not know about crossing the Gulf in a single. Many pilots do it, but I do not know. As for the rest of it, I might have had a few anxious moments, but I am sure I would have gone.

How much is it worth to avoid a few anxious moments? We loved the Baron. It gave a sense of well-being in the damnedest places, and as light planes go, it is a powerhouse. The day came when it had to go. The beast was eating us out of house and home. We sold it and bought a single, a Beechcraft Bonanza, which could do just about anything the Baron could do, except fly with one engine out. I flew the Bonanza over the most rugged areas of Colorado and, as it happened, over more low stratus decks on a particular flight than I ever did in one flight in the twin. Frankly, it did not bother me. I never even noticed the other engine was not there. I guess it is because deep down I know that those engines never quit.

IX

Learning from Students

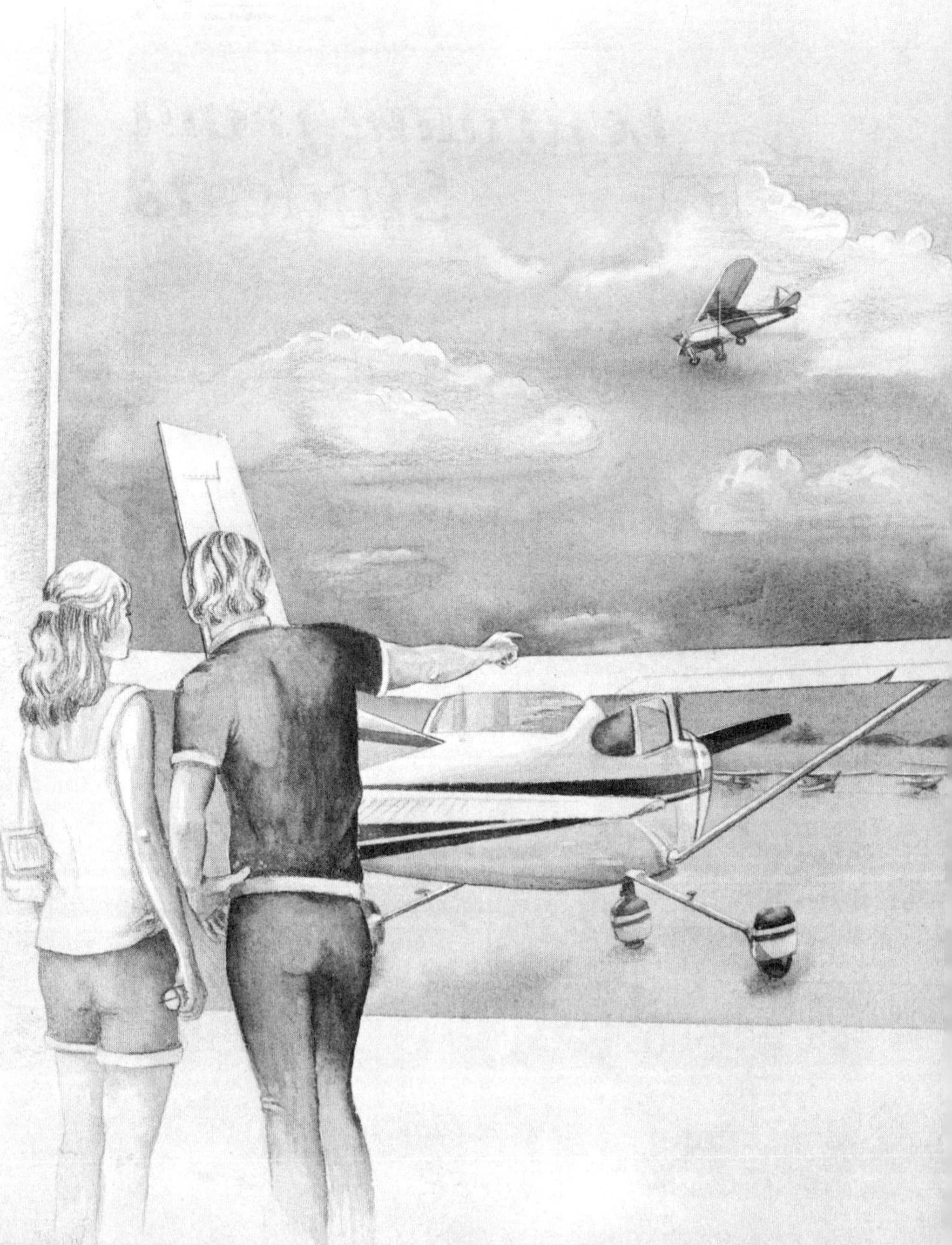

Exactly why I decided to get an instructor's rating I do not remember, if, in fact, I ever knew. I had always enjoyed learning, but instructing had never appealed to me. Learning is a painful process, but a challenging one, and dependent for the most part on nothing but the student's own determination. It can be frustrating and discouraging, but the dividends are good, particularly when the subject is flying in any of its various aspects. Flying light planes, either as a means of getting somewhere, or as a means of relaxing by going nowhere, has been pleasurable, but rarely as stimulating as those episodes spent in exploring some new dimension of the art of flight.

About fifteen months and almost sixty flying hours after my first instruction, I completed a check ride that entitled me to a private license. This license bestows the right to carry non-paying passengers in weather good enough to permit visual flight. I alternated trips like this with periods of instruction or solo practice designed to earn a commercial license.

As grounds for pursuing such a course I couldn't advance the slightest logic. I never intended to, nor have I ever, charged the first dollar for carrying a passenger or any cargo, the only practical reasons for obtaining a commercial license. At the time, 1971, the chief qualification for obtaining a commercial license was a proficiency in executing spirals, lazy eights, pylon eights and other similarly almost-pointless maneuvers, which may justifiably be compared to practicing scales on the piano. Many successful, competent, and eminently sensible commercial pilots have pursued lengthy careers in aviation without ever performing such maneuvers after earning their commercial license.

So I continued to fly passengers without pay, still in relatively clear skies, pleased with the knowledge that I could charge them if I wanted, and unperturbed by the fact that they probably wouldn't go if I did. As before, these trips were alternated, this time with sessions under the hood and an instrument instructor in the right seat. I was working toward an instrument rating.

The trips with friends were pleasant. For some reason the practice under the hood was more satisfying, perhaps because I could see a goal. Maybe it was the thought that I would get another piece of paper at the end of the course. It would be a useful one, for it would entitle me to hook into the nation's air-traffic-control system and fly directly to my destination, through clouds if necessary, rather than around or under them.

The day came when I got the instrument rating. For the first time, the airplane became a significantly more reliable and occasionally even a practical machine. It added a new dimension to the satisfaction of cross-country flying. Of even more interest to me was my initiation into the complexities of multi-engine flight, which I started within a week after passing the instrument check ride.

The addition of the multi-engine rating on my license left a predictable void in my life, despite the purchase of a half-interest in a twin-engine Piper Apache. Perhaps to an impartial observer it may have seemed that I was afflicted with an obsession for collecting certificates, as though the paper were an end in itself. Perhaps. But for many pilots there is little that the world of flight has to offer that matches the drama of the first excursion into some unexplored realm, mastering a new terrain. For some of us, I believe, the experience of learning is rarely equaled by what comes later, gratifying though much of it may be. I sometimes wonder if there is another endeavor in which proportionately so much time is devoted to sharpening skills as compared to the time spent in using them. Some pilots may spend two or three hours, and some twenty to thirty, staring at instruments under the hood, or practicing spirals or chandelles, simple turns or takeoffs and landings of all types—for every hour spent traveling or sightseeing. It is not true of all pilots, but of enough to make one wonder whether the phenomenon has a parallel elsewhere.

This, I suppose, was the nature of the void that I felt after the multi-engine check ride. For over three years during my initial venture into flying I was a student. For over two years after returning to it I remained a student. Now I felt lost. Flying to another part of the country was an adventure. But something was missing.

It was that something missing that lured me into learning to be an instructor. Less than a year after the multi-engine rating came my first venture into aerobatics—ten hours dual instruction. That was not my last such flirtation with this sport, for I have returned to it sporadically over the years. I don't know why I don't practice aerobatics more, or why I haven't dropped it altogether. On the one hand it is more challenging and more deeply satisfying than almost any other phase of flight to loop or roll a plane, to fly it inverted, to change course by means of an Immelmann, or to fly it straight up into a near hammerhead stall. On the other hand it is expensive, uncomfortable because of the unaccustomed G forces it produces, tedious in the necessity for the straps and harnesses of the parachutes, and frustrating in the wait for the rare days of sufficiently clear weather required for such unorthodox flight.

Sooner or later, exciting as it is, one gets the premonition that one loop will become a loop like all others, one roll like all the rest, and that the world in time could look as familiar with the sky below and the earth above as it does the other way.

I would never demean the fulfillment that comes with continued practice and increased precision, or at least proficiency, either in aerobatics or in the less-extreme maneuvers—the eights, the spirals, the stalls, and even the simple turns, takeoffs, and landings. But even continued practice and proficiency is not a substitute for the newness of that long-ago first flight, first landing, first solo, first cross-country; or the first flight into clouds, or the first loop.

The instructor's certificate did not tempt me. I would learn nothing new. A candidate for the instructor's rating learns no aspect of the art that he has not learned before. He learns to do it from the right seat rather than from the left. He learns to explain it, both on the ground and in the air. He is told the common errors in each maneuver and how to critique a student's efforts.

I held back. The instructor who was to teach me the course discouraged me. He was the same man who so enthusiastically taught me the aerobatics. He was a highly skilled professional who took an infectious delight in flying. To him, as to me, it seemed pointless if I really did not intend to instruct. But I went ahead with it anyway, more as a means of increasing significantly my own proficiency rather than in the hopes of exploring anything new.

There were times when I felt I would have been better advised to listen to my own and my instructor's better judgment. Becoming a certified instructor did not at times seem worth the effort. Flying to distant parts of the country, Mexico, and the Bahamas in the Apache, and later in the Baron, offered more and was certainly newer than the fundamentals of flight that I was now relearning from the right seat of a single-engine trainer.

Still, I persisted in my possibly pointless quest. I alternated the cross-country flights with sessions with the instructor, and approached them with almost as much enthusiasm. Perhaps it was because no one gave me a certificate at the end of the cross-country flights. After eight months, and a little over twenty hours of dual instruction, and written tests in the principles of flight and in the fundamentals of instruction, I took my check ride with an FAA inspector.

It was a tough check ride, the toughest I have ever taken. This wasn't because it was for the Certified Flight Instructor's Certificate, but because I just happened to get that kind of inspector. He was a good one; bitingly critical, but good. He had been weaned in the Army Air Corps, as they called it in his day, and he reminded me of the flight instructor in every bad wartime movie about flying I had ever seen.

I knew what kind of ride I was in for when, after doing a few turns, he told me very matter-of-factly that he guessed I knew that my coordination was not the best. Actually I knew no such thing. I always thought my coordination was pretty good, but I had seen too many movies to argue. My first landing, he told me, was "pretty sloppy for an instructor." These were the *com-*

plimentary remarks. When he wasn't "complimenting" me, he cajoled, grimaced, criticized, barked, and—most humiliating of all—grabbed the controls to demonstrate various maneuvers.

By the time we were through I had long quit thinking about the CFI Certificate. Somewhere about halfway through the ordeal, I began to fear for my license and the right to fly at all. I imagined him not only denying the CFI Certificate to me but revoking my own license and grounding me for thirty days, if not for good. Some time later in the ride I decided not to contest the revocation since I no longer felt safe to fly solo, let alone to risk the necks of passengers.

As we taxied back to the FAA building he broke the silence with the reluctant comment that he was going to "write my ticket," though I obviously had a lot to learn. Then he muttered, half aloud, as though musing on uncounted personal experiences, a two-part statement, one part of which I have found to have no substance, the other half of which I have found to contain the profoundest wisdom: "When you start teaching, those students will teach you to fly; they'll try and kill you."

That was over seven years ago. Since then I have given over 700 hours of instruction, most of it to primary students—not an impressive figure by professional standards, but enough to justify some tentative conclusions.

No one has tried to kill me, not even figuratively speaking. Except perhaps during my first few hours of instructing a new student landing for the first time, I have never experienced while instructing the gnawing feeling in the pit of my stomach that all pilots experience sometimes. It is a feeling that sometimes accompanies the sight of a line of thunderstorms across one's path, or an important instrument's going haywire, or the realization that a checkpoint has not shown up as it should have. I have felt it often, but never while giving flying instruction.

There still seems to linger here and there the picture of the student freezing at the control, grabbing the stick with a superhuman grip, born of terror, and plunging earthward with his helpless instructor. I guess such things have happened. I don't know when, under what conditions or why. Many students are afraid; there's some apprehension in almost all of them. Fear keeps many potential students away from flying, but fear, I am convinced, brings many others to the airport for lessons. The fear itself is a challenge. For more than a few students and licensed pilots the first solo or the private certificate represents the conquest of a deep-seated fear of flying.

You can often spot such students the first time they grasp the controls, no matter what history they may relate or what reason they may give for being there. In some, the tension is constant; in others, manifest only at certain times. I have seen and felt it, not only at obvious times, such as the demonstration of a stall, or the unannounced throttling back of the engine for a simulated forced landing, but also at less expected occasions. These include the sudden appearance of light turbulence or the change in engine speed that results sometimes from slightly more severe chop. This latter occurrence can sound for all the world as though another plane has sidled close by.

I have never known a student to "freeze" at the controls. I have difficulty imagining such a thing and even more difficulty imagining that I could not wrest away the controls with my own hands and my own voice should it ever happen. Perhaps in the World War II "two-holers," where instructors sat in the one seat of the tandem two-seater, it was more likely. I don't know. I only know that in the very few instances of real panic I have seen, the students did not seize the controls. Rather, they threw their hands in the air and pleaded for help.

I have taught each of my four children and a number of other people to drive automobiles. Cars make me very tense. I do indeed get a bit nervous teaching someone to drive a car and I feel that my nervousness is entirely justified. This is not only because of the lack of the dual control that takes much of the sting out of flight instruction, but, more important, because danger lurks at every corner. Driving a car on the city streets does indeed require constant exercise of quick reflexes. Danger to life is a clear possibility at every major intersection or along any busy street with a novice at the wheel. Even a drive down a narrow one-way street means the constant danger of a fender bump or a sideswipe.

There isn't much that can happen at two thousand feet in the air. There is no loss of control that cannot be corrected, and other air traffic poses no serious problem. Bank the wings to get a better view of the sides; turn to check below and look around. If there is nothing there, you can be certain that another craft will not dart from behind a building at a blind intersection, nor is there much likelihood of any student, no matter how inept, careening into a telephone pole through misjudgment of dis tance, nor any danger of a student sideswiping a plane that suddenly darts out of oncoming traffic to pass. Despite the admitted necessity for complete awareness of other traffic, midair collisions are extremely rare and the potential need not precipitate the constant adrenaline flow that accompanies the venture into city traffic with a student at the wheel.

I find instructing one of the most truly relaxing endeavors aloft. It is physically untaxing and untiring, except on the voice, and most of the mental faculties are freed for observing the student.

The first landing may be the only exception. Alertness is required. Ground looping can occur quickly, following a sloppy landing and an ineptly attempted recovery. The new instructor soon learns that minimal correction suffices. The challenge to most new instructors is not to learn when to take over the controls, but how to keep hands and feet off them.

To learn to use the dual controls at his disposal to smooth out an impending rough landing is almost instinctive. To learn not to takes longer. Sooner or later the instructor learns that once the craft is flared at approximately the right height above the runway at approximately the right speed, there isn't much that can happen that will endanger the safety of the occupants, and almost as little that can really damage the plane. The steel-spring main gear of most trainers can take a terrible beating. They are built that way. The nose gear often takes a bad beating too. Unfortunately, the oleo-strut nose gear is not built for it, and most trainers must be taxied with the controls aft to keep the weight off the badly shimmying nose wheel. A shimmy in the nose is the price the fixed-base operator usually has to pay for renting out a trainer. More serious damage to the structure from hard landings is rare.

It is tempting for the instructor to straighten out with the kick of the rudder the nose that is about to touch down at a crab angle, but the student will have to feel the resultant side load on the gear if he is ever to learn why he must do that himself. It is tempting for the instructor to turn the aileron control to stop a side drift caused by a crosswind, but this too must be avoided for the same reason. Only when the crab or the drift is extreme, or to prevent an off-runway landing or a potential ground loop, is the instructor justified in interfering. More difficult is resisting the urge to yank back the control to prevent the nose wheel from smacking into the ground, before the mains, in the wheelbarrow-type landing. Sometimes this too must be suffered in the cause of effective teaching.

It is true that instructors on occasion have been maimed and killed by their students. It is true that insurance to instructors for instructing costs more than other forms of flight insurance. Perhaps I have been fortunate in my students, but my instincts tell me that instructing is not in essence a dangerous endeavor. I have learned to relax with students as I would on a cross-country trip over flat open land on a clear day. It may be a fool's paradise but I have come to enjoy instructing very much. My students haven't tried to kill me.

But only that half of my check pilot's parting words to me were wrong. In the other half of his statement he was entirely correct, and I have had many occasions to think of them. The students have taught me to fly—I am sure, in this feeling, I am not unique. I'm sure that other instructors have been taught by their students and not taught by being forced to grab the right seat controls to avoid an imminent disaster—that is the least of it.

The most of it is that I saw students making mistakes or having difficulties with various maneuvers and I blithely explained what I had come to assume was the correct explanation. I have seen students conscientiously follow my instructions and have seen the problems remain. So, I have had to think, and have had to pull dusty books and manuals off the shelf. I have had to do some reading. I have at times had to do some serious reflecting and even a little agonizing. I have at other times been forced to the realization that the accepted explanations and sometimes even the sacred script of the flying texts are not completely accurate, at least not to my thinking.

I have realized on occasion that this or that procedure or maneuver I have learned through practice to do almost instinctively. But I have also realized at times that what I learned has little relation to what the books have said I must learn in order to do it. Instructing students forces one to think, not only about particular problems, but about the entire learning process. Perhaps in this respect teaching flying is not different from teaching any other skill.

I, as a new instructor, tell my new student: "Coordinate the rudder and the ailerons going into or coming out of a turn." The plane is turned by use of the ailerons; moving them causes the wing to bank and the plane to be lifted around the turn. We use the rudders only to prevent the drag caused by the downward-deflected aileron on the high wing from causing the nose to skid toward the outside of the turn.

I tell the new students to use the rudder with the aileron simultaneously and to the same degree. They do. But it rarely works with new students. I figure their coordination must be bad, but I soon realize it isn't that at all. I try it myself. I try to notice what I do that keeps the ball centered and our derrieres firmly in our seats. Sooner or later I realize that in a right turn I need more rudder than aileron and that in a left turn I must lead with the aileron. Not by much, but enough so that my instructions were not working. It becomes obvious to me that the propeller, turning clockwise as seen from inside the plane, and the left-yawing tendency that it causes when the plane's equilibrium is disturbed, come into play more than I realized, more than the books explained.

This requires a delay in bringing in the left rudder when starting a left turn, and it requires greater right rudder going into a right turn than left rudder going into a left turn. It is a small point. Sooner or later the student will instinctively learn to make smooth turns no matter what I tell him, but "greater right rudder in a right turn," and so on, seems to help and saves him from moments of self-doubt about his own coordination. He has learned more quickly to make a smooth turn and we can more quickly move to something else. He has learned something, but I think I have learned even more.

I learn also because students have questions. Usually they are satisfied with my answers, but sometimes they are not. Sometimes I am not. I look at the books. My dissatisfaction is often well founded. Sometimes it is because my own understanding has been inadequate; at other times I have been completely wrong. Occasionally, the books are no help, but my own reflection convinces me of the inadequacy of the answer. Sometimes my own fumbling attempt to articulate an answer in the plane, or just after landing, is enough to convince me that I need to think, or read.

For the most part, these questions are not about obscure aspects of complex areas. The frequency and the relative simplicity of most questions that cause trouble are sometimes disconcerting, sometimes almost humiliating.

A new student taxies out for takeoff. He has already gotten the knack of steering with the rudders rather than with the automobile-type wheel that controls the aileron, as almost all new students first try to do. That having been mastered, I explain, as I have to all students before him, that while taxiing into a quartering headwind the wheel should be turned and held into the wind. While taxiing with a quartering tailwind, the wheel should be held slightly forward, turned, and held away from the wind. My student, a well-educated insurance executive of about thirty, startles me with a single question: "Why?"

Inwardly I am angered. I suspected from the beginning that this man was compulsive, that he had to know everything at once. He probably suffers from an anxiety neurosis. Why doesn't he just do what he is told? We have more important things to talk about. In time it will become "obvious" to him, second nature.

I mumble something about keeping the wheels more firmly on the ground, about keeping the weight off the nose wheel, and offer only a cursory attempt to explain either the how or the why. My student nods and seems to understand. He can't possibly. I made the explanation and I didn't understand it at all.

I console myself with the recollection that as a student I accepted the instruction and never pestered the instructor for an explanation. Then a voice says: "Dumbo, you should have."

I look at the manuals. All of them explain in detail, complete with diagrams, how the controls should be held while taxiing. Remarkably, only one of them gives any explanation of the reason. I do better by talking to several more experienced instructors, only a few of whom seem really to understand or able to explain. The next time around I tell my student in more detail the reasons for the use of the controls while taxiing. I merely want to make sure he understood, I explain in the most casual manner. In an even more casual manner he nods. Apparently he has put this subject behind him. He is now more concerned by two or three other questions. He had obviously been doing some thinking of his own.

I am not always wrong—even when I am nagged by self-doubts, sometimes it happens that I am right.

A very bright woman student will not keep the ball centered during a tricky maneuver taught to all students, the "takeoff-and-departure stall." It is a stall executed with full power intended to simulate the consequences of an excessive nose-high attitude upon take-off by a pilot oblivious to his diminishing airspeed. The left-yawing tendency at such low speed and high power is very strong. Without sufficient pressure on the right rudder, enough to keep the ball centered, a vicious power-on spin can result.

"More right rudder," I repeat on each successive maneuver. "Center the ball." The ball does not center. There is not enough right rudder being applied. She gets angry. She is pressing it all the way, she says. It doesn't matter. If the ball doesn't center, it is not enough.

I feel the incipient spin, take the controls, lower the nose, back off on the power, and tell her to try again. She gets angrier. She will never learn with my flying the plane, she complains, and maybe she is right. Maybe I should let her go.

So I let her go. The ball hangs out to the right; the plane shakes. I feel the spin coming but I do nothing. The ball stays out; the nose stays up—till suddenly it drops. The plane spins wildly—I do not remember in which direction. The student says nothing, but the panic is there. It is in the desperate unspoken plea for help, as she takes hands and feet off the controls and looks at me. I take the controls, back off the power, release the pressure and stop the spin with the rudders.

We try it again.

This time there is no need to take the controls. The ball stays in the center. She completes the stall and recovery. We have both learned something.

A male student practices slow flight in a Cessna 152, essentially a Cessna 150 with an additional 10 horsepower. But it seems to have a more ready disposition than a 150 to spin from slow flight with insufficient right rudder. Slow flight is another instance of an aerial maneuver that is like practicing scales. It teaches familiarity with the control pressures and responses at the lowest speed at which the plane can be controlled. The lowest speed requires high power, full flap, and a high angle of attack. Once again the ball want to slip out to the right.

The problem with this student is the same as that of the woman. He does not complain, but I get tired of hearing myself say the same thing over. I decide to keep quiet. I have never had a student spin from slow flight and again I decide to let things take their course.

The spin comes suddenly, as do all power-on spins. His panic, unlike the woman's is vocal. Unfortunately, he does not get over it quickly. He asks to go back to the airport. The next time up he asks my indulgence while he just flies around to relax in the plane and I oblige. The next time after that he goes with another instructor. Whether he continued to fly I do not know.

A pre-med student has trouble holding altitude during 30-degree bank turns. So he starts to stare at the altimeter trying desperately to stop the loss of altitude. The bank steepens while he stares at the altimeter. I suggest that he look outside, that the natural horizon and its position in the wind screen is the best indication of whether he is losing or gaining altitude, and that it will tell him at the same time if his bank is steepening.

He tries to follow my suggestion but the lure of the altimeter is too strong. The temptation to check the altitude is too great.

He looks at the instrument; the bank steepens until I forcefully call his attention to it.

It is the same story: he continues to repeat the same mistake, I butt out. I decide to become an interested spectator and to see if I have been too concerned. Maybe he will correct the bank on his own.

It is an interesting show. The bank steepens, the nose drops. My young friend pulls back on the controls. The turn tightens. He has 45 degrees of bank. If he looked up, the sharp angle of the horizon would probably startle him, but he does not look up; he is glued to the altimeter. At this stage of his new career he has not learned a proper instrument scan. He has not yet been taught the folly and the danger of staring at one instrument.

He rolls in more trim to keep the nose up. Momentarily it works, but the bank steepens and the nose drops farther. The speed increases. I have read of such things happening in clouds, but here is a real demonstration in bright sunshine and I am totally absorbed. The speed is about 110 mph. Normal speed for a 30-degree bank turn in this trainer? Maybe 90 mph. He notices neither the excessive speed nor the excessive bank. At 60 degrees of bank the speed has passed 115 and is moving to 120. The altimeter is unwinding. Still he comes back. The airspeed fluctuates wildly, down to 80, as he pulls back, then quickly builds to high numbers, with just the slightest relaxation of the controls as the steepening bank loads up the plane with G forces.

As we approach 70 degrees of bank I feel it has gone far enough. I tell him to look up. He is shocked. Instinctively he rolls the plane level. Instincts do not help a novice out of a spin, instincts are all wrong for that situation. But instincts do help him out of a spiral, if he sees that he is in one. My student had only six or seven hours of training but the plane returned to normal flight in seconds, almost automatically.

Teaching, for me, has been extremely lucrative. There have been frustrations, but they have been worth it. I feel I have unexpectedly earned a small fortune.

Namely, I have relived time and again the experience of learning to fly, one of the more gratifying experiences of my life. I have been permitted to share the experiences of others, similar to mine in some respects, and in other respects quite different. My own quest was postponed to a later age than I ideally would have wanted. It is never too late, of course, and there are no doubt advantages that come with increased age, experience and maturity, but they are bought at the price of youthful enthusiasm and quick reflexes. Some might call it recklessness, but the verve with which some younger men take to the controls of a plane makes me envious that my own obsession was not satisfied at that age, and makes me curious to know how it might have been. It is little wonder that the military forces, when they can be choosy, choose youth.

Young, old, or somewhere in between, however, in one form or another students experience the same emotions. Only the degree is different. The reactions, the handling of the problems, and the outward responses of the individual students are different, but the emotions that cause them are much the same. You learn this from watching them in the plane and from talking to them over coffee. There is some fear in the outwardly most calm. There is often a deep enthusiasm and a fascination in the most outwardly tense or nervous. Observing it all is similar in a way to an aerial view of a town you have spent some time exploring by walking the streets. I have walked the streets of the places where the student is exploring. When the same spark is there, I do not need to be told.

I suppose there is another reason for it all. Maybe I am like the pedagogue who would rather teach simple arithmetic to young children than to study calculus for himself.

The natural progression in the higher education of the part-time aviator begins with a transition from a two-seat, 100 hp trainer, with one navcom and a fixed-pitch prop, to a four-seat, 150 or 200 hp job with two navcoms. Perhaps there will also be added a few other gadgets such as a transponder and an automatic direction finder.

Then comes variable-pitch prop and retractable gear, and cowl flaps to permit better cooling on the ground and during a climb. Next comes distance measuring equipment and perhaps autopilots to keep the plane level and on a constant heading.

Couplers that connect these automatic pilots to the omni follow shortly, along with an altitude hold so that the pilot will be completely free to press buttons and will not be distracted by having to keep his hands on the controls at all. Then come couplers that link it up to the ILS so that the autopilot flies the approach.

There follows in short order a sophisticated device known as area navigation. A computer is hooked up in some magical way with distance measuring equipment and the omni. The owners proudly explain that with this you can "move" the omni station so that you can track to any point you want by punching in the radial off the omni station and the distance that the point is on that radial that you want to track to. This is followed by altitude-encoding transponders that automatically give your altitude to the ground controller. He can read it on his radar scope and does not have to trouble to ask you for it, and you do not have to be bothered to tell him.

As the pilot's experience and earning capacity increase, come flight directors that save him from having to fly the craft himself during a transition from one phase of flight to another and save him from having to feed in different information to the computers during flight. It is all done at once.

It is very exhilarating to many of the breed. Every nook and cranny of the panel is crowded with electronics. The more automation the better. Twenty percent of the cost of the entire machine can be in the electronics. Forty percent of the time may be spent in the electronics repair shop. It doesn't matter. Pilots boast of their long flights by autopilot without touching the controls the way the early birds boasted of battling thunderstorms or fighter pilots of dogfights.

One pilot compares his X32Y40 radio package with the K-21 glide scope and RNAV, all coupled to a Q49073 autopilot to another man's R420N6 package with electronic digital readout and needles that move straight across rather than swinging from a point. You would swear from the pride in their voices that they invented the gadgets themselves.

The whole subject bores me. Worse, it deflates me. I revel in an instrument approach, actual or simulated, flown with reasonable accuracy to the decision height. Then I am told with glee of the marvelous autopilot that flies the craft precisely, untouched by human hands. I spend hours on cross-country flights making a game of keeping the omni needle reasonably near center while holding the altitude at a close approximation of that assigned by air-traffic control. Then I am told, with awe, of the unerring autopilot and the unwavering needles and altimeter.

I think that is one of the reasons that I took to aerobatics. None of my airport friends have yet boasted of the precise loops or rolls executed by their beloved autopilots. I do not doubt that the wizards of the industry could produce one that could do loops or rolls or anything else if there was any point to it. Happily, there is no point to it. So from time to time I retreat to aerobatics and I am spared the deflating experience of comparison with the gyroscopic automaton.

The other escape from automation is, of course, the student. He glories in mastering the turn, the climb, the descent, slow flight, the instrument approach—all with his own reflexes, coordinations, perceptions, and responses. A well executed 360-degree turn accomplished by the hands and feet of a live pilot still seems more satisfying than the marvels of modern electronics. I can relate to the joy of the student in mastering these simple maneuvers. To the joy of the pilot in the precision of his plane's robots I cannot.

So I stick with the students through climbs, turns, descents, stalls, landings, chandelles, lazy eights, instrument flights, and approaches. Until one day he is ready to get down to business, to put it all to use. Until he buys a plane, and a DME and an automatic pilot with omni and ILS couplers and area navigation, and maybe radar and a flight director.

Then it is time for me to go do a few loops, hammerheads or Immelmanns to shake out the cobwebs. Or to get another student and start all over.

X

In Search of a Reason

Is there nothing to be said for the light plane as a means of travel? Have the problems posed by jet traffic, weather and mechanical and electronic equipment rendered the machine no more than an expensive toy? For the expenditure of so much effort and wealth by a handful of weekend pilots in almost every community in the land there must certainly be more justification than local sightseeing and sport flying.

Is it perhaps a quiet, smooth, comfortable ride, unrivaled in any other mode of transportation?

Not really. Light planes have comfortable seats, but seats from which you cannot rise or, as a rule, even stretch your legs fully. In this latter respect, the flivver's are perhaps no worse than most airline seats. But at least in the liner you can stand upright and walk down the aisle if so inclined. In all but the most lavishly expensive light planes, you cannot stand up and there is no aisle to walk down even if you could. There is no place to walk to even if there were an aisle. There are no lavatories on light planes, except for those few designed only for millionaires. Some planes have long-range tanks that do nothing to solve the problem of short-range kidneys. Those who want to make full use of a 4½- to 5½-hour fuel capacity bring along a gadget known as a relief bottle.

Smooth? Often, but not as often as the ride in a jet which is above much of the weather that causes the bumps. With the exception of a rare but sometimes severe high-level phenomenon known as clear-air turbulence, the jet passenger faces far fewer bumps per mile or per hour.

Quiet? Not on your life! The marvels of modern engineering have been unavailing against the deafening roar of blades beating against the air at a rate of over 2,000 turns per minute—at least when the blade is mounted to a plane with the limited weight-carrying capacity of light planes. Most of these small craft are too flimsy to be airtight, and the wind whistling through the cracks and crevices adds its din to the props and the engine. The "super soundproofing" advertised by the manufacturers is a farce, even when the plane is brand new. With a little wear, any slight reduction in sound is lost. The plane simply cannot bear the weight of real soundproofing.

Pilots will tell you that it does not bother them and that you get used to it. According to scientific studies, you get used to it when you start to lose your hearing, as you inevitably do if you fly light planes for several hours a week, every week, over a period of several years. Fortunately, a very simple solution is available. A decent pair of earplugs costs only a few dollars, cuts out the top level of the sound and brings it down to something bearable and tolerable even over long periods. It permits easier comprehension of radio transmission and passenger conversation, and decreases tremendously the fatigue factor that results from the continual, oppressive beat of the engine and prop.

Unfortunately, however, most pilots really have become used to the noise and really are not aware that it actually does bother them, whether they know it or not. Perhaps the use of the plugs is simply not compatible with their image of a pilot. They will forego the silk scarf and goggles, most of them, but they will not wear earplugs. I would rather save my ears for better things—I wear the plugs.

So what *do* you get for it all? Freedom of scheduling? Convenience? Access to small fields at small towns where the liners do not go? Perhaps. But do not examine those propositions too closely.

The fact is that the scheduled departures of the liners between cities of any size are generally close enough for anybody's needs. What about the burgs and villages that you must reach by transferring to another plane, or by renting a car at the nearest town served by the airlines? If you look hard enough, you will sooner or later find two small towns, the distance between which can be traversed by light planes quicker and easier than by the airlines, or by a combination of airlines and rented cars.

We were in Burlington, Vermont, and planned to stop in Charlottesville, Virginia, on the way home. For amusement and curiosity, I checked the airline scheduling while killing time at the terminal, and found that with their transfers in New York or Richmond, I could make it quicker in my Baron. I noted also that we would not even have been able to begin our journey from Burlington until considerably later than we had planned. Such situations are not usual. They exist, and there are times when the four- or six-seater is a very practical and efficient means of transportation. They are rare. I know that many pilots and all light-plane manufacturers claim the contrary, but I think they are rare nonetheless.

The freedom of leaving when you want, of taking the route you want, of stopping where and for how long you want, the privacy—I would be one of the last to minimize these. But these are personal considerations and their worth is very subjective. Try and prove any of it with figures in minutes saved—you cannot, except here and there and now and then.

Can you prove it in dollars? Is it cheaper? Yes, under certain conditions. Those conditions include a pilot-owner who does a lot of traveling that he would have to do with or without the plane, enough traveling to keep him airborne for approximately 300 hours a year. Even then the saving is questionable, unless one or more of the passenger seats is filled most of the time with persons who would also have been traveling by other means.

Under other circumstances, it is cheaper only for those who like to compute only their direct costs: gas, oil, and tie-down fees; and figure that they have the fixed costs to pay whether they take their plane or not. Owning a plane is cheaper, in other words, if you like to kid yourself.

For what most light-plane owners pay yearly for the purchase, maintenance, insurance, reserve for engine overhauls and hangaring, they could buy a leisurely trip for two for anywhere from fifteen to sixty days depending on the plane, to anywhere in the world. The more financially sophisticated of them try all sorts of gimmicks—lease-backs to flying schools or fixed-base operators, formation of flying clubs, and the like, and consider themselves fortunate to cut the expense even a little bit.

You do not have to be rich to own a plane, but you cannot be poor. Some owners, however, quickly get poor after buying their bird. Try as they will, except in very few instances, there is no way a pilot can financially justify owning a small plane no matter how many business trips he makes or how many he convinces the Internal Revenue Service he makes.

There are presumably some few doctors, lawyers, contractors, salesmen, and businessmen for whom a plane is a necessary tool and a financial boon. I do not think I have ever known one. They are rare enough to rate articles in flying magazines from time to time for their uniqueness.

Fixed costs are high. The more you fly, the more you spend for fuel but the less you spend per hour of flying time when you figure it all up at the end of the year. You can easily go broke flying enough to keep the hourly cost low. The accepted dogma among the weekend pilots is that only a fair-sized business corporation can have the continual need for light aircraft that justifies a plane as a business tool. They look with envy at the corporate executives and owners who fly their own planes, presumably saving money as they do. These types love to explain to their hangar friends how indispensable the plane is and how much they save with each flight.

Perhaps they believe it themselves. Perhaps they really do save. I am more inclined to believe a level-headed, nonflying accountant friend who told me, after many years in the business, that he had yet to see the books of a corporation whose plane really paid for itself. After many years he was convinced that the boys up front wanted it for pleasure, adventure, prestige, or ego. Call it what you will, it was something that was not showing up positively on the corporate books.

I think he was right. Fortune 500 corporations undoubtedly have a legitimate need for a plane or a fleet of planes. For most others, the airlines and rented automobiles are, together, too reliable, too economical, and too available to justify any claim of the economic necessity for a light plane.

For those who do not fly enough to justify owning a plane, renting one is not much better. Costs are high. Unless you are going and coming right back most operators want to charge something for "down time," and there is still the problem of ground transportation when you get where you are going. Depending on the number of people making the trip, and the distance involved, it is a rare jaunt that will economically justify the rental of a light plane. The practicality of using the plane is squeezed from the short end by the economy of auto travel, and from the long end by the economy of airline travel.

No, I think the manufacturers have sold us a bill of goods. After all the charts and figures and the convincing prose, for at least 90 percent of the non-professional pilots—whether they fly in connection with business, or go only on vacations, or use the plane for both—there is little economic justification for any of it.

Why then do we fly? What justification is there for a noisy, confining, rather flimsy machine that can match the car or the airliner for neither economy or reliability?

Perhaps there is no justification, but perhaps there doesn't need to be any. Most of those who spend every spare hour and every spare nickel on those infernal machines cannot answer the question, nor do they even ask it, even to themselves. They do not understand it when it is asked by others.

To the pilot, flight is an end in itself; it needs no further justification. To make your trip in your own plane, or even a rented one, is a triumph. To have to abandon the flight plan and drive, or take a commercial flight, is a defeat. No matter how sensible or necessary the decision may be, it is a defeat. Pilots, most of them, are the first to commend a brother pilot for his good sense in leaving the plane tied down because of threatening weather, shaky electronics, or incipient engine problems. No matter. It is an experience lost—it cannot be made up. The same route can be flown at a later date, but it will not be the same flight. No two flights are ever alike. The weather, the winds, and the traffic conditions at the destination airport are never exactly the same. It was, if nothing else, a chance to be airborne for a few hours, and there is no way to recapture it.

Pilots do not ask each other why. They hang around the restaurants, pilots' lounges, hangars, or briefing rooms, waiting for the clouds to lift, the thunderstorm to move on, the mechanics to adjust the magnetos or the gaps in the plugs, or the radio man to get the black box talking again. All this for the sake of another hour or two aloft.

Pilots do not ask, but nonpilots do. The question is not always direct. It is often unspoken but implicit. As often as not the pilots' boasts of the incredible performance of their planes and of time and money saved is an answer to the unasked questions. Like anyone else, when confronted with a question to which there is no answer, or to which the answer is not readily perceived or is impossible to explain, pilots tend to lie, sometimes even to themselves.

On some of the few occasions when I have been directly asked, I have reacted with involuntary and unwarranted hostility.

"Why do you fly?" asks a lady tennis buff in casual conversation at a social gathering. "Why do you play tennis?" is my immediate and irrelevant answer. Although I have seen similar defensiveness in other pilots, I reflect on such answers with regret. I really should apologize.

Lady, I am sorry. I would tell you why I fly if I could, but I cannot. It is just too difficult to explain, especially over drinks in a noisy hall.

A word in mitigation: it is not only our own inability to explain that makes us so fiercely defensive. If some of our crowd appear boastful and arrogant, there is some extenuation.

There is defensiveness in others, and hostility. There is an ill-defined suspicion in those who fly that the others do not really need to ask why, that they understand at least as much as we do. The urge to get a view of the world from above, or to find your way to the next town through the air, rather than over the ground, is universal. We have seen too much evidence of it to doubt it. In most, it may be neglected or repressed, perhaps sensibly and justifiably, but it is there nonetheless. This is not something that afflicts only a few.

I do not solicit either students or passengers, except those who have first volunteered an interest. I do not look for converts to flying. I do no missionary work. But I have continued over the years to receive, from time to time, rejections to invitations that were never extended. People who would never tell me that they would not set foot in my home, even should they happen to feel that way, will volunteer that they would not set foot in my plane.

It is an interesting phenomenon. There are pilots who refuse to admit to themselves that they fly for the sheer love of flying, who invent all types of practical justifications for it, and feel threatened when questioned about it. There are those others, nonflyers, who refuse to admit the inherent lure of flight because through fear, inability, lack of opportunity, or other valid reason, they have had to repress it and feel threatened by our very presence.

That they would not set foot in a small plane doesn't disturb me. I don't need any nervous passengers. There are too many who are too eager to satisfy a deep, long, and lingering curiosity about flight in its elemental, pristine condition; flight on a human scale unadulterated by pressurized cabins and jet engines that breathe best at 30,000 feet. I do not look for such passengers, but would never refuse them.

Sometimes on long cross-country trips, or in quiet reflection on the ground about such things, there reappears to me the outline of a face and the form of a man I saw from a distance at the airport in Wichita Falls, Texas. It was a gray, overcast, drizzly day. The thick stratus layer extended all the way past Pueblo, Colorado, our destination, to the front range of the Rockies. There were no ice and no thunderstorms, just a solid layer covering much of that part of the country. It was as though a kindly fate had put it there just to give me a chance to fly instruments for two hours without wanting to concern me about severe weather. I suppose to the casual observer it was what could be called "bad weather." To me it was not bad at all. I looked forward to entering the cloud deck as someone else might look forward to the comfort of a warm blanket.

As Isabel and I walked out to the plane through the light drizzle, I looked over to the other side of the field and saw a line waiting to board a prop transport plane, which belonged to one of the smaller airlines. It was a typical line of people. Groups of two or three were talking to each other, and the rest were looking straight ahead at their own plane, waiting for the door to open or for a signal to start boarding. All except one man, who was staring across the field directly at us.

When we reached the twin-engine Baron, Isabel climbed aboard while I went through the ritual preflight inspection. After checking the fuel and oil, I started to walk around the bird to give it a last, casual once-over. Unconsciously, I looked across at the line of passengers in the distance and saw the same scene. The same man was still staring at us. I climbed into the cabin and went through the starting checklist, and started up each engine. As I opened my charts to place them on my lap, I looked again. The line was starting to move, but not my unknown friend. He was still staring.

I monitored the automatic terminal information service for weather, wind and active runway information, and then received taxi clearance from the airport ground control. As I swung the Beechcraft around to taxi, I gave one last look at our strange observer. He was walking slowly forward, still looking squarely at us as other passengers passed him by. I felt his eyes on my back as I taxied out and wondered as I took off if he were straining through his tiny window aboard the transport to watch us.

As best as I could judge, he was a man of middle age. From that distance I could tell little else. That he was staring at us, there could be no doubt. That was clear even from a distance. Why he was doing so, I could not know.

Perhaps he thought we were insane to be taking off in such a small plane in what may have looked to him like such bad weather. Perhaps he just wondered what kind of people would fly in a small plane at all. Perhaps he was a private pilot himself and simply enjoyed watching someone go through a familiar routine. But I do not think so. He was much too absorbed and I do not think he was watching anything familiar. I think the scene entranced him because I think it awakened a long-forgotten urge to master the controls of a plane in flight. I think that probably at one time, before he put such thoughts to rest as impractical and unproductive, he was like the small boy who watched us taxi to our parking area at Charleston, West Virginia, then called after me through the airport fence: "Mister, how long does it take to learn to fly?"

I am sure that whatever twinge of envy was included in his protracted study of our movements disappeared shortly after we left his sight. It disappeared because he had, undoubtedly, experienced nothing, or too little, of the world of flight that lies within a few thousand feet of the surface. Without some frame of reference even the most active imagination is powerless.

The world that our distant observer probably never saw is beyond the reach of most travelers. It has been left behind by the denizens of commercial aviation. By those who make their fortune flying passengers and cargo, the lower atmosphere has been abandoned. It is now the stomping ground of the amateur, the sportsman, the adventurer—those for whom flying is a hobby or an avocation. A little, very little, commercial flying is done in our domain.

For this we are not unhappy. This is our part of the sky. From a few thousand feet up, the surface can still be recognized as part of the planet we live on, and there are riches that can be extracted only from those who fly low and slow.

There are, for one example, those calluses on the face of the landscape, the blotches that we call cities. The sight of a clearly discernible skyline on the horizon demands attention at first only because it marks a destination or a checkpoint. The steel and glass spires serve first only to show the way, like any other inanimate object. Only as it grows larger do you see evidence that it is a thing alive, only when you see the blood vessels and arteries from all points of the compass merging into the center of the scar tissue. There is a sameness to all of them, and a uniqueness to each.

A city taking shape in the distance is always interesting, but it is not always attractive. Flying to Mexico City at Christmastime, we found the air crystal-clear at 12,000 feet. From the front seat of the Piper Apache, my companion and I could see the twin peaks of Popocatepetl and Iztaccihautl towering over 17,000 feet, from at least a hundred miles away. We knew they were south of the city, but our search of the vast plateau ahead of us for the first sight of the metropolis was distracted by a huge yellow cloud in the distance. It lay there in marked contrast to the light, fluffy puffs that drifted just a few hundred feet beneath us and, obviously, it could not really be a cloud.

We wondered if it could be a grass fire, but decided it covered much too large an area. The fact that my needles were guiding us directly to it prompted a more careful look until I could make out the silhouette of the sprawling city at the bottom of that yellow mass. The reported Mexico City visibility of only three miles on this beautiful clear day should have been a clue. As a sight from afar, it was an interesting study, but I hesitated to descend into that murky mass. Other trips in the spring found more haze in the mountains, which at least tended to camouflage the sharpness of this layer of pollution.

Far different was my first glimpse of New York City from the cabin of a light plane. A cold front had preceded us, clearing all the junk from the air over the northeast coast. Philadelphia was stretched out 9,000 feet below us, an absorbing sight indeed. But looking far into the distance, about seventy miles to be more precise, was what appeared to be the south shore of Long Island and to the west a pinpoint of land that had to be Manhattan. Isabel and I kept it continually in sight and witnessed a growing panorama as more and more of it came into our view and details emerged. The twin towers of the World Trade Center, the buildings of central Manhattan and Wall Street, followed by the Verrazano Bridge, over the Narrows, Governor's Island, and the Statue of Liberty. As we descended along the Brooklyn side of the East River for the approach to La Guardia, the entire island lay to our left, wide open to inspection, baring every secret. We had watched that monster city grow from a dot on the horizon to its full, overpowering presence, and I can't recall a more thrilling twenty-five minutes aloft. Three other flights to New York City have each offered their own rewards, but have failed to match it.

As the first sight of American civilization to greet the lower-atmosphere traveler returning from the Bahamas or the Carribean, Miami is a jewel of a city. Its multitude of gemlike structures are set artistically against the various shades of the waters of the Atlantic and Biscayne Bay. The trees are as intriguing as the forest. Take off from Miami International Airport and turn north along the shoreline. Stay a half mile or so out over the water at no more than a thousand feet up. Fly past mile after mile of glittering hotels, swimming, pools, beaches, patios, and sun terraces; wonder at the endless variation in shapes, sizes, colors, and designs in which luxury is fashioned. Even for those who have no desire to savor its pleasures, Miami Beach is a continuous spectacular show to the light-plane passenger.

Cities at night become different creatures. One twinkling light on the horizon grows to millions of individual pinpoints of an infinite variety of patterns and color. The cumulative glow reflects off the base of cloud covers and off nearby lakes and rivers. During the day, these waters are different colors. At night they are all black velvet.

Coastlines are a particularly intriguing study from the air, whether it is the stark, deserted 240-mile stretch of the almost ruler-straight line of the Mexican east coast between Matamoros and Tampico, or the never-ending array of bays and inlets of the Florida Panhandle. The universal lure of the water is never so evident as from the air. The evidence is seen over many miles of coastlines and on almost every navigable lake that may pass beneath your wings. It takes the form of wooden shanties and palatial homes, small settlements and rows of hotels, apartments and condominiums, each hugging the water and sprouting into it a pier or a dock. The wakes of small motorboats and large yachts can be spotted long before the craft themselves, and on any clear day on any body of water of any size one can see a harvest of sails.

The water itself is a study in color variation. Flying east from New Orleans along the coast one can tell almost precisely the boundaries of the dumping ground of the Mississippi River. From the mouth of the river, almost due south of Gulfport, Mississippi, it leaves the water a muddy gray to the Alabama-Florida line. It almost looks as though the river had reached a working agreement with the Sunshine State to keep hands off her blue and green waters. Westward from New Orleans, I have followed the coastline as far as Tampico, Mexico, but do not recall such a well-defined change.

The Bahamas have an appeal of their own. The islands themselves, with their varied shapes, each a lush green trimmed in white, seems to have been handmade; but the waters of the Bahamas are a chameleon. They change their colors, light green to dark blue, gradually, except where abrupt changes mark the presence of a coral reef. The surface-bound tourist sees but a small part of the riches that surround him. None of these views can excel the last few miles of the approach to Bimini, with its unparalleled view of the ocean's bottom through the clear water adjoining the island.

Are these sights oases in a desert? There are those who say so. Flight was defined long ago by at least one professional pilot as hours of boredom punctuated by moments of stark terror. In recent times terror has faded into the background, but many passengers would redefine flight as hours of boredom punctuated by rare moments of visual fascination. Those rare moments are the ones that reach out for the air traveler: the sights are too overwhelming to be ignored by even the most blasé. There are infinitely varied and continual, if more subtle, sources of fascination in the changing face of even the most ordinary landscape.

Until you first glimpse the Rockies, when flying west from the Mississippi River or its environs, for example, the terrain offers no mighty spectacles. No single feature reaches out for the attention of the casual passenger. On most routes across the central third of the country, there is not even a mountain range to break the monotony. The ranges and canyons that do exist, mostly in the southwestern part of this area, are unspectacular. Only after you have spent most of a day traversing the entire breadth of it, does there emerge an awareness of the hidden drama of that landscape.

One who travels by auto westward to the Rockies from Chicago, St. Louis, or New Orleans starts from flat land near sea level. He terminates his journey about five to six thousand feet higher, on land almost equally flat or amid gently rolling hills.

Except as an item of curiosity, the altitude means nothing to him. Altitude to him means height above the ground, not above the sea.

It is different by air. Take off from New Orleans, or any of these cities on or near the river; climb to 8,000 feet above sea level, a good cruising altitude for most unturbocharged light planes, and you are approximately 8,000 feet above the ground. The ground itself is flat and gentle. It is mostly green and dotted with lakes and laced with rivers. As you fly west you become aware of a gradual drying out of the land and of gentle swells in the landscape. The change is gradual, but enough to be noticeable.

By the time you are over Goodland, Kansas, things begin to happen faster. You seem to be closer to the ground, and you are. It is only a little over 4,000 feet beneath you, though you are still at 8,000 feet above sea level. The visibility is often excellent. You can see everything, including the contours of giant thunderstorms that spring up around you in that area on a summer afternoon. There is reason to be grateful that the ground rises to give you a better look. Some consider it a dull ride, but, if such a thing is possible, there is a curious fascination in its very dullness.

The land is flat and the roads are straight. There is no reason for them to curve in western Oklahoma, Kansas, or eastern Colorado. There are no hills or large bodies of water to block their way. Half of the roads parallel each other and cross the other half at right angles—or so it seems—laying out a giant grid across the land. Within the large squares are farmlands, smaller squares or rectangles. There are no forests or woodlands that break the patterns.

Where the roads intersect, there are towns, and in all of them a steeple. In many of them the steeple is at the intersection of the highways. I have on at least one trip to the mountains made a game of looking for a steeple at the crossroads in each town; and I saw one more often than not.

Within many squares, or rectangles, are large circles of plowed ground. A friend from Kansas City explained to me that it is better protection against the wind. It is only this circular plowing that breaks the monotony of the straight lines and right angles.

By the time you are ready to start your descent at Colorado Springs, or Cheyenne, you are made forcefully aware of what has happened, for you do not need to start down until you are quite near the field. The ground at Colorado Springs or Cheyenne is only 2,000 feet beneath you; at Denver only 3,000 feet. By the time you approach central Colorado or eastern Wyoming, it is difficult not to notice the entire ground boiling over near your own altitude, for boiling is what it seems to be doing. The rolling hills of the grasslands are a green liquid. It is a storm-tossed sea that froze at the height of the fury—a green ocean that suddenly solidified when the swells were at their peak. Or so it seems. Geologically, I know nothing about it. I only know that if you look at these giant swells long enough they seem still to be in motion.

I have read that this gradual rise of 6,000 feet in the elevation of the land from the Mississippi to the Rockies, unbroken by mountain ranges, is an occurrence unique among the land masses of the world. I have no trouble believing that. The facts and figures of this phenomenon and its geological history and causes can be found, no doubt, in geology books. The drama of it can be experienced in a light plane. I can imagine no other way.

It is not only a very subtle experience in itself, but if you intend to continue westward, a stark contrast to what lies ahead.

What lies ahead is neither subtle nor gradual. It is a walk among the most awesome array of mountain peaks found in this country or Mexico. Beyond Denver lies the front range, whose peaks thrust here and there about 5,000 feet above the valley floor to a modest 11,000 feet above sea level. Beyond them is a valley drained by the Arkansas River, the northern part of which is itself almost 10,000 feet above sea level. Beyond this valley lies the towering range of snow-capped peaks known as the Great Divide.

Over a score of these giants top 14,000 feet. The ridges themselves are frequently over 12,000 feet, and the entire mass gives pause to the light plane pilot from the East wanting to do battle with it.

There is a mountain in California that is slightly higher than any of them. I have never flown in that state, but the contour lines of the map show nothing to equal the rugged line in west-central Colorado. There are a number of volcanic peaks in Mexico that arise far above the level of this Colorado contingent, but they are isolated and scattered widely throughout the country. The Colorado Rockies dominate the domain that is the upper practical limit of the capacity of light planes.

Above 12,000 feet, the performance of the unturbocharged engine falls off sharply. The nose of the aircraft points noticeable higher because the wings must take a bigger bite out of that thin air just to maintain level flight. They must meet the relative wind at a higher angle. The airspeed reads low. Continue on up to 15,000 or 16,000 feet to top the peaks, if you dare, and you are soon balancing on the edge of the precipice. With full power available, your airspeed at level flight soon approaches that magical number, a low number, known as the best-rate-of-climb speed: to go faster is to descend, to go slower is to descend.

The performance of the pilot without oxygen decreases also at these altitudes. Though this decrease is not as predictable, the one who chooses to top those peaks without breathing supplemental oxygen does so at his peril. It all depends on age, physical condition, use of tobacco, and other factors. The effects are insidious; there is a feeling of well-being, a total lack of apprehension, but a marked decrease in mental alertness and response, whether noticed or not.

Some men need the mask anytime they are over 12,000 feet; others only if they are there for at least an hour. The regulations require it for the pilot over 12,500 feet for over thirty minutes and over 14,000 feet the entire time. I do not doubt that pilots who live and fly there daily get along very well without an oxygen mask most of the time.

A need for the mask may also depend on the pressure you are under. The first time I tried to thread my way through that maze of valleys I stayed safely at 14,000 feet to avoid all but the highest peaks. The narrowness of the lower valleys did not appeal to me. I was looking for Aspen, approaching from the north on a return flight from Jackson Hole, Wyoming. I got lost, completely lost. The all-powerful omnis are useless there. Their signals are blocked by the mountains. There is no omni station within forty miles of Aspen and the signals are intermittent and unreliable. You navigate by looking at the ground and sometimes at the compass. I flew up one valley and down another trying to correlate the map to the ground, awestruck by the gold, white, and green that surrounded me. Foolishly, I snapped pictures with a camera in one hand as I groped my way, until I stumbled upon Aspen by accident, by trial and error.

On the ground, reviewing the morning's mistakes, I was overwhelmed by the number of clues I had missed and the elementary procedures I had ignored. A year later, breathing through an uncomfortable oxygen mask, it was easy—everything fell into place. With greater familiarity with the area, such a high degree of alertness is not required and I have later had no problems even without the mask.

Most planes from the lower country do not come equipped with oxygen systems and one must be rented if needed—not always a simple matter. Equipped or not, most light planes are unwilling to go to these heights. It is a struggle to get the machine up there, and it obviously does not want to stay. If your destination is Aspen, Glenwood Springs, Salida, or any one of the other fields nestled in narrow valleys, you have to descend into the valley to land; you might as well stay to begin with down where the air is denser, and you and the engine breathe better.

But to tackle the Great Divide, you cannot stay too much lower than the peaks, since there *is* nothing too much lower. You soon see that as you cross the Arkansas River Valley.

If you are flying to Aspen from the south, from Pueblo, for instance, you fly north along the valley's western side with the awesome mass of the Great Divide to your left. You scout the mountains looking for a low spot, a way of easy passage. There is none. Every yard of this range defies the challenge. You know from the map that the only way in or out of Aspen or Glenwood Springs from the south is by way of a relatively smooth 12,000-

foot-high valley floor that treads its way between the peaks. It is known as Independence Pass.

The entrance to the pass from the east is marked by a reservoir known as Twin Lakes and it is guarded on each side by snow-capped sentinels of over 14,000 feet. The one on the north is Mount Elbert, the highest point in Colorado. As you approach the rocky ridge, you cannot wait too long to climb; the rate of climb is slow at these altitudes, sometimes agonizingly so.

On a wall at the Aspen airport is a map. There are many pins stuck into the map, each pin representing a point where a light plane, at some time over the years, has collided with the terrain. There are a distressingly large number of them. The old timers say that most of them are "flatlanders" from "back East." A disproportionate number of these pins are in the vicinity of Independence Pass.

There is much literature published by national aviation organizations, Colorado pilot groups, and by the FAA, advising flatlanders about mountain flying in Colorado. Most of them contain a statement such as, "Flight through Independence Pass is not recommended," or something similar. They advise an approach from the more gentle country to the north. Even more strongly do they advise a departure from Aspen to the north, which avoids the abrupt climb necessary to clear Independence Pass from the 7,800-foot-high Aspen Airport. Their motives are good—this advice is based on experience and it is hard to quarrel with good motives and experience.

But what this literature recommends avoiding is an overpowering scene of indescribable grandeur. The flight from Pueblo to Aspen by way of Independence Pass is the most awesomely beautiful flight of its kind in the country. "Of its kind," includes any flight across the Great Divide such as that from Denver to Ogden, Utah. The landscape of Independence Pass is more intense, the sheer number of the peaks more overwhelming.

There is a dialogue between the tiny plane and the giant rocks wherever they meet at these levels. The pilot feels that neither the ground, nor any portion of it, should intrude in this domain, which belongs exclusively to the world of flight. It looks grotesquely out of place to see the ground at such levels. But then you look at the sharp edges that the wind and ice have carved into the granite, and you wonder for how many thousands of years those rocks have been honed. You learn the meaning of the word "antiquity." This is *their* domain, and these rocks in the sky and their tricky currents of surrounding air were there long before there were any men to dream of flying past them.

There is a threatening aspect to it all. You listen to the beat of the engine, and its steady roar sounds as though it is mocking the danger below, but then you look again at these peaks and wonder: Will *they* have the last laugh? It would take weeks to find the wreckage.

You tread your way carefully between the peaks as the narrow pass rises higher and higher toward your level. Only at its highest point is it smooth enough, wide enough, and level enough to permit a possible emergency landing. Only during those few minutes at the crest can you absorb without distraction the shattering impact of your closeness to these wild mountains. I have never petted a lion, but I suspect the experience is similar.

If you are landing at Aspen, the descent begins as soon as the pass starts falling away on the west side of the range. The pass narrows, requires more alertness. A misstep may put you in a blind canyon, but no apprehension or exercise of caution can undermine the impact of this magnificent array of stark beauty.

It's over too quickly. The range is too narrow. I have often thought that one day I would like to spend hours flying back and forth across the pass. Better judgment will probably intervene.

There was a time when a drive by auto through mountainous country was a pleasure to me, but I'm afraid these flights have ruined it. After five flights to the western part of the country, including three across Independence Pass, I finally had the occasion to spend a few days driving through some of the highest parts of the Rockies. I did not drive through Independence Pass, nor did I have any desire to. The drive that I made was frustrating enough. The alternate dips and climbs of the road as it hugs the mountainside, the infrequent views as you twist and turn from one peak to the next, or from one row of them to the next, are a poor substitute for the endless vista, the continually changing panorama and the easy stride from each snow-capped peak to the next.

A flight across 600 miles of water offers rewards of a different kind—they gratify a curiosity that can be appreciated by anyone who has stood on any shoreline, looked to the horizon, and wondered. It didn't matter that hundreds fly every week from New Orleans to Merida in the Yucatán Peninsula of Mexico in an hour and a half at 30,000 feet in air-conditioned comfort. I had seen too many enticing glimpses of the Gulf of Mexico to resist the lure for long. One morning, after waiting to hear from the National Weather Service that storms in the Gulf had moved safely eastward, two friends and I climbed aboard the Beech Baron and headed South to Merida. For close to two hours on this three-and-a-half-hour trip, there was no one on the ground to talk to and no omni signal. We were out of range of Grand Isle, Louisiana, and of Merida.

When I figured us to be about seventy-five miles from the Mexican shore, the omni picked up the Merida station. I watched the needle quiver and finally come alive, a sure indication that land was breaking the horizon, if only the haze did not blur it so. From seventy-five miles, however, even at 10,000 feet, land was not to be seen. We strained our eyes looking for the shoreline of a peninsula. The barely perceptible line breaking the horizon through the tropical haze was as unaccountably electric as if we had crossed an uncharted sea.

Neither the sight of land, nor the quivering omni needle, were the first incidents to quicken the pulse on this journey. A hundred miles off the north shore of the Yucatán Peninsula lies an island of coral about 20 miles in length, the Arrecife Reef. It appears on the aviation charts, but its bare outline on the chart is no hint of its appearance from the air. We were totally unprepared for the spectacle of colors that lay below us, a fascinating spectrum built of the remains of untold millions of microscopic creatures accumulated over how many millions of years. Why? And why there?

There are but a few of the shapes dimly perceived by those for whom the silent stranger from Wichita Falls is for me the symbol. The list is endless. There is Mount Rainier, the perpetual guardian of Seattle, which I saw towering far above my flight level, its lonely 14,000-foot mass rising from a 2,000-foot plain, its white crown jutting through a halo of clouds that would have made it invisible from the ground; the sight of the Pacific Ocean from the crest of the rugged mountains of Southern Mexico's west coast; Salt Lake City spread out suddenly 6,000 feet below as you cross, at 11,000 feet, the lowest ridge of the Wasach Mountains—a city trapped between mountains and the Great Salt Lake. There are bridges, monuments, rivers, canyons, expressways, traffic jams, and fog banks that cover parts of cities, leaving other parts clear. They are all part of the dividends.

When clouds blot out the land and everything on it, the show is not over. The clouds themselves are not the least of it. The same landmarks, the same terrain, always look the same; the same patch of sky always looks different.

I remember flying to Houston one evening at dusk. My course took me between two towering buildups of near-thunderstorm proportions. They were both too awesomc to tangle with, and in the fading light, I looked cautiously to both sides lest I get too close to either of those dark masses. But as I passed near the western side, there was no more difficulty in seeing them—they glowed like lightbulbs from the reflected light of the setting sun. Darkness was all around except for the glow of their boiling tops.

Summer afternoon buildups are always avoided as much as possible. Some are benign, some are malignant. You can't always tell by appearances. In some, no water has formed; in others, the plane gets a thorough washing and you find out if the fuselage leaks and, if it does, where. Through the vents you feel alternately warm air as the plane involuntarily rises, perhaps a thousand feet a minute, and cold air as you uncontrollably descend.

The flat field of solid cotton below may have ripples indicating turbulence, or it may be like white satin, generally signifying none. The fields of white may be hypnotizing and lead you to believe that they never end—then will surprise you by ending abruptly, like water at a shoreline—revealing unexpected vistas of the ground. The clouds may imperceptibly rise and ultimately envelop you. In such cases, you look at your altimeter as the whiteness comes to meet you, for you feel you have been absent-mindedly descending.

When your altitude fortuitously keeps you skimming across the top of a stratus deck or near an endless field of scattered cumulus puffs, there is an exhilarating sensation of speed totally lacking in level flight, except the level flight of daredevils, who buzz or skim the surface of the land. The dizzying backward motion of the clouds beneath or around you, however, has none of the perils that attend the maneuvers of the low-flying barnstormers.

There are painted sunsets, rainbows with a brilliance, a clarity, that belong exclusively to those who view them in their own habitat and night skies over wilderness areas, star-studded beyond the recollection of those who grew up in modern cities.

Is it the promise of experiences such as these that bring us to the airport despite the risk, the delays, the aggravation and the expense? I doubt it. It is important to some of us, the hint of it attracts more. I doubt it alone holds many. It is more of a fringe benefit.

There are those who love planes and flight to whom the view means little. They are preoccupied with performance, airspeed, fuel-consumption, stability, or other characteristics of the plane or its equipment. They take little note of what's beneath them, and I can understand that, for I myself would swap almost any vista for a chance to fly instruments. For me, the most entrancing aspect of flight is not the scene below, but those episodes when temperature and dew point come together and leave me enveloped in a domain in which there are only needles and dials, a domain in which there is no below, no above and no outside. The most exciting view of the ground for many of us is still the end of the runway as it emerges through the haze after a well executed instrument approach.

Why do people fly light planes? Some no doubt to satisfy a curiosity, others to look for something to do, an interesting pastime. The high drop-out rate among flight students attests to the emptiness of the reasons, or the aimlessness that brought them to the airport in the first place. Flying is not for them and they do not generally persist. Their curiosity or their need for achievement is satisfied by the first solo or the private license. They experience little of the world of flight.

As for the rest, those who stay and willingly devote to flying a respectable chunk of their lives, what are their reasons? Except for the few who earn their living by flying, or for whom flying serves a practical need, flight is an end in itself—it needs no justification. To say this, however, means nothing. It only raises more questions and invites more speculation.

Some think flying is a death wish and say that small-plane pilots are under some strange compulsion to duel death and to see how close they can come without losing. I have known one or two such pilots. They are strangely out of place among the rest of the airport crew. The daredevil is not held in awe nor respected. Most serious private pilots are not ashamed of their fear of the weather. They boast of their prudence. To boast of one's fearlessness is the mark of an outsider, a novice, or a dilettante. I do not know how it was forty years ago, but that is the way it is today.

Others claim, and I suppose still others believe, that there is a desire to prove one's manhood involved in flying, a desire to prove one's self, an element of machismo. This is a well disguised factor, if it exists. I have detected little, if any, resentment directed to the growing number of female pilots or to their obvious equality in adeptness, coordination, skill, and general mastery of flight. Most pilots, consciously or otherwise, believe that anyone can fly—if he or she wants to.

I have been asked on at least one occasion, by a nonpilot, if a lengthy flight I planned was to prove that I could do it. I answered that that was not necessary, that I could prove that with pencil and paper alone. I don't know if my answer was understood by my well-meaning, but uninformed, friend.

Why then, do we fly? For myself, there is only one honest answer: I have no idea. Perhaps flight, like music, expresses emotions too deep for words. Perhaps, it is all too pointless—not everything has to have a reason.

Nor do I have any idea of what the future holds for aviation. There is talk of super jet ports many miles from the large cities. Passengers will be whisked to them by monorail. There is talk of hypersonic planes that will go over 2,000 mph at over 100,000 feet. There is talk of rocket planes, and so on. It would be comforting to say that no matter what comes, this little world of private flight will always exist in some small corner of the airport or in fields vacated by the giants of commerce. It would be comforting too to say that we will continue to fly our increasingly outmoded machines, low and slow, in the lower atmosphere long since abandoned by everyone else.

Unfortunately, I have no way of knowing that. "Always" is a long time. The fact that private flying has survived the incredible progress of the last fifty years intact is no guarantee for the future. There are many who say we are a menace to safety, that we interfere with "important" flying, and that the skies are full of single-engine planes with pilots having heart attacks and just missing collisions with 747s.

There are more and more regulations controlling flight in more and more of the sky. There is talk of user taxes, and there are increasingly more types of mandatory equipment and requirements of all kinds.

Pilots, however, are a bellicose bunch when their little kingdom is threatened. They accuse the rulemakers and the tax collectors of trying deliberately to overtax us and to regulate us out of existence. In magazines and meetings, private pilots advance all manner of practical advantages that render their continued existence essential. I read their articles and feel uneasy. Must our existence depend on practical need? If we are not needed, must we go?

Nonetheless, I do not think we will. I think that no matter what the future holds for aviation that there will, indeed, be a small group of pilots on the other side of whatever kind of airports there are, or in some kind of fields somewhere, talking about the age-old issues that have interested pilots since the Wright brothers. They will tinker with their machines and watch—and, when necessary, wait—for the weather to change, just for the sake of another hour or two aloft on weekends.

If there are forces trying deliberately to destroy private flying, they will find that it will not go quietly. If it is in the cards, however, for private flying to go the way of the Stanley Steamer and the zeppelin, and if we cannot survive the inexorable changes of time, I suppose that all of the protestations and arguments will not avail. The real rewards of flight that is low and slow do not show up in the books at the end of the year. They are such that they do not count for much these days.

If it comes, our passing will be little noticed or lamented. It will rate a back-page obituary, but no front-page coverage. It will make too little difference to most people. Private flying is too much like the faceless citizen who pays his taxes, supports his family, and obeys the laws, but makes no waves or great contributions to society. Perhaps private flying's demise will not be a national tragedy, but one more preserve that is noble and unique will have passed from the scene.